THE END OF THE REPUBLIC
AND THE DELUSION OF EMPIRE

THE END OF THE REPUBLIC AND THE DELUSION OF EMPIRE

by

James Petras

Clarity Press, Inc

© 2016 James Petras
ISBN: 978-0-9972870-5-9
EBOOK ISBN: 978-0-9972870-6-6

In-house editor: Diana G. Collier
Cover: R. Jordan P. Santos
Cover image: U.S. Secretary of State Hillary Clinton gestures with Libyan soldiers upon her departure from Tripoli in Libya October 18, 2011. Photographer: Kevin Lamarque. With permission from Reuters.

ALL RIGHTS RESERVED: Except for purposes of review, this book may not be copied, or stored in any information retrieval system, in whole or in part, without permission in writing from the publishers.

Clarity Press, Inc.
2625 Piedmont Rd. NE, Ste. 56
Atlanta, GA. 30324 , USA
http://www.claritypress.com

TABLE OF CONTENTS

Part One: Presidential Elections

Introduction *11*

Chapter 1 .... *15*
Clinton and Trump:
Nuclearized or Lobotomized?

Chapter 2 .... *28*
Democratic Party Primaries:
"Progressives" as Political Contraceptives

Chapter 3 .... *42*
Presidential Elections 2016:
The Revolt of the Masses

Chapter 4 .... *50*
Trump "The Fascist":
Backdoor Backing of Political Psychopath, Hillary Clinton

Chapter 5 .... *56*
Plutocrat-Zionist Support for Hillary Clinton

Part Two: The Delusion of Empire

Chapter 6...*65*
Anglo-America:
Regression and Reversion in the Modern World

Chapter 7...*82*
The Mote Remains in the Emperor's Eye

Chapter 8...*97*
President Obama:
The Race for the Imperial Legacy

Chapter 9...*111*
Global Economic, Political and Military Configurations

Chapter 10...*120*
The International Monetary Fund's Rogues' Gallery

Chapter 11...*124*
Wars:
US Militarist Factions in Command

Chapter 12...*148*
Mandarin for the Warlords:
The Harvard School of Empire Building

Chapter 13...*161*
A Critique of CFR's "Revising US Grand Strategy toward China"

Chapter 14...*172*
Western 'Mainstream' Media Extremism:
The Lies of Our Times

Part Three: Leftists and Islamists

Chapter 15..*187*
The Left:
Business Accommodation and Social Debacle

Chapter 16..*198*
Twilight of the Idols:
Rise and Fall of the Personalist Left

Chapter 17..*204*
Past and Present Islamist, Democratic and Nazi International Brigades

Part Four: Zionism in America

Chapter 18..*212*
Zionist Power:
Swindlers and Impunity, Traitors and Pardons

Chapter 19..*229*
The Jewish Policy Elite in the United States:
Meritocracy, Myth and Power

Index..*248*

To my inspiration and wife
Robin Eastman Abaya

and my comrade, scruffy Sophy

INTRODUCTION

"The world we live in is at a dangerous point right now. We are in the grip of a dangerous project by ideas that we call neo-liberalism that have brought us to near catastrophe."
Ken Loach accepting the Palme d'Or at the Cannes Film Festival 2016

2016 is a year for living dangerously. The events—the Presidential elections and their political consequences—can profoundly affect the prospects for nuclear war or peaceful accommodation, the status quo or electoral upheavals.

Worldwide, elites strive to deepen the reversal of social welfare, while across four continents, millions of workers mobilize to retain and advance their social livelihood.

The political foundations for America's global military dominance are under siege by insurgent voters confronting a highly militarized power elite headed by psychopathic war mongers.

The Presidential elections are everything 'abnormal'. The principal Democratic candidate, Hillary Clinton, has indicated her willingness to nuke Iran for Israel and to direct missiles to Moscow and Beijing.

America has launched full-scale wars in four continents. In the Middle East it bombs Afghanistan, Pakistan, Yemen, Iraq, Syria, Libya, and Somalia. In Asia American war planes and battleships approach China's coastline. In Europe guided nuclear missiles are surrounding the Russian heartland.

America has seized the moment to regain its stranglehold over Latin America. Political proxies have seized power in Brazil and Argentina by electoral chicanery and coups. Military intervention in Venezuela is on the agenda. President Obama's imperial "legacy" is pursued and can be calibrated according to the number of social programs revised by vassal regimes.

The End of the Republic and the Delusion of Empire centers exclusively on the immediate dangers that are erupting and moving inexorably towards continental and regional realignments. It addresses in a broad brush, the existential choices confronting the American people and their government—whose hopes and desires pull in opposite directions.

Four major upheavals face America in 2016.

1) The US Presidential primaries, for the first time, included a democratic socialist backed by tens of millions of voters, who openly challenged the power and prerogatives of Wall Street. The Republican candidate leads a mass rightwing revolt which opposes globalization, capital flight and the free entry of immigrant labor. Not since the New Deal, nearly a century ago, have class relations come into sharper confrontation.

2) Not since World War II has nuclear war drawn the US and Russia closer to mutual annihilation

due to US empire building. The Presidency, in pursuit of a global legacy, draws on the support of the extremist mainstream media, prestigious Harvard mandarins of war, and military factions to achieve global hegemony, even as rebellious working peoples resist, and Russian and Chinese adversaries rearm and advance.

3) Year 2016 is also a time of rising popular insurgencies confronting the bankers, the warlords, and their political proxies in America. Popular movements in France, Spain, South Africa, Argentina and Brazil, call for popular revolutions. The traditional Social Democratic, center-left parties, through accommodation, have been ousted by workers or co-opted by elites. Under the pressure and duress of capitalist wars and greed, mass electoral upheavals, general strikes, and armed resistance openly challenge the empire.

4) The fourth critical issue that faces America's year of decision, is the question of who rules America and who sets the military agenda in the most contentious regions of the Middle East? An organized neoconservative policy elite reflecting Zionist influence has gained ascendancy under dubious claims of meritocratic credentials. Their economic policies have plunged the country into repeated crises, systematic swindles and spiraling inequalities. Equally, the Zionist foreign policy elite has plunged America into prolonged, losing wars resulting in disastrous human and financial losses. The political and economic power of

the Zionist configuration has severely repressed critical debate and political action which challenges Zionist dominance.

The End of the Republic and the Delusion of Empire is about the American empire and its wars and injustices, and its adversaries, the peoples worldwide and in America who oppose it in pursuit of egalitarian, democratic republics.

PART ONE

PRESIDENTIAL ELECTIONS

| Chapter One |

CLINTON AND TRUMP: NUCLEARIZED OR LOBOTOMIZED?

Introduction

Over half the US electorate views the two leading candidates for the 2016 Presidential elections with horror and disdain.

In contrast, the entire corporate mass media, here and abroad, repeat outrageous virtuous claims on behalf of Hillary Clinton and visceral denunciations of Donald Trump.

Media pundits, financial, academic and corporate elites describe the prospects of a Clinton presidency as one of responsibility, national security, business prosperity and political normalcy. In contrast, they paint billionaire Republican candidate, Donald Trump, as a grave threat, likely to destroy the global economic and military order, polarize US society, and destined to lead an isolated and protectionist US into deep recession.

The super-charged rhetoric, flaunting the virtues of one candidate and vices of the other, ignores the momentous consequences of the election of either candidate. There is a strong chance that the election of ultra-militarist Hillary Clinton will drive the world into catastrophic global nuclear war.

On the other hand, Trump's ascent to the US Presidency will likely provoke unprecedented global economic opposition from the corporate establishment, which will drive the US economy into a profound depression.

These are not idle claims: The destructive consequences of either candidate's presidency can best be understood through a systematic analysis of Clinton's past and present foreign policies, and Trump's belief that he has the ability to transform the US from an empire to a republic.

Clinton on the Road to Nuclear War

Over the past quarter century, Hillary Clinton has promoted the most savage and destructive wars of our times. Moreover, the more directly she has been engaged in imperial policymaking, the greater her responsibility in implementing foreign policy, the closer we have come to nuclear war.

To identify Hillary Clinton's path to global war it is necessary to identify three crucial periods. Hillary's bloody history can be dated initially to her de facto 'joint Presidency' with husband Bill Clinton (1993 – 2001).

Stage One: The Conjugal Militarist Presidency (1993 – 2001)
During Hilary Clinton's joint presidency with William Clinton (the Billary Regime) the First Lady actively promoted an aggressive militarized takeover of Eastern Europe, the Balkans, the Middle East and Eastern Africa— often under her favorite messianic doctrine of humanitarian intervention and regime change.

This justified the relentless bombing of Iraq, destroying its infrastructure and blockading its population into starvation while preparing to carve its territory into ethnic and religious divisions. Over 500,000 Iraqi children were murdered, as proudly justified by then-Secretary of State

Madeline Albright (1997-2001) and lauded by the Clintons.

In the same manner, the US humanitarian coalition air forces and their cruise missiles bombed Yugoslavia over 1,000 times from March 24 to June 11, 1999 in the course of sub-dividing the country into five backward ethnically cleansed mini-states. Thousands of factories, public buildings, bridges, passenger trains, radio stations, embassies, apartment complexes and hospitals were devastated; over a million victims became refugees while hundreds of thousands were wounded or killed.

The conjugal presidency successfully carried out the bloodiest war of aggression in Europe since the Nazi invasion during WWII, in order to subdivide an ethnically diverse and industrially advanced federation whose independent foreign policies had angered the Western corporate empire.

The Clintons launched the military invasion of Somalia (in East Africa) to impose a vassal regime, leading to the death of many thousands and a regional imperial war. Faced with desperate popular resistance from the Somalis, the Clintons were forced to withdraw US troops and bring in thousands of Sub-Saharan African and Ethiopian mercenaries—whose deaths would pass unnoticed by the US electorate.

From 1992 through 2001 the Clinton war machine helped set up the Yeltsin kleptocratic vassal state in Russia, facilitating the greatest peacetime pillage of state resources in world history.

In the post-Soviet breakup era, over 1 trillion dollars of former public assets were seized, especially by US and British-allied Zionist gangsters, Clinton-affiliated officials and 'academics,' and Wall Street bankers. Under Clinton's vassalage the entire Soviet public health system was eliminated and Yeltsin's Russia experienced a population decline of 4.3 million citizens, mostly due to diseases, alcohol and drug toxicity, suicide, malnutrition, unemployment, loss of wages and pensions, and an unprecedented epidemic of tuberculosis and infectious diseases once thought wiped out, like syphilis and diphtheria.

Senator Hillary Clinton: War Crimes by Association— January 3, 2001 to January 21, 2009
During the George W. Bush dynastic regime, Senator Clinton supported the US war machine 'sowing death and destruction to the four corners of the earth' (to quote Bush Jr.), during which millions in Iraq and Afghanistan died or fled in terror. Bush had only deepened and expanded the mayhem that the Clinton conjugal presidency had begun a decade earlier.

Senator Clinton promoted the US direct and unprovoked invasion and occupation of Iraq and the war in Afghanistan. Senator Clinton embraced crippling economic sanctions against Iran and she blessed Israel's military assault against Palestinians in the West Bank and Gaza and Israeli massacres in Lebanon.

Senator Clinton supported President Bush Junior's aborted coup against Venezuelan President-elect Hugo Chavez (2002), a prelude to the coup attempts in Latin America that she directed later as US Secretary of State.

Hillary Clinton's Senatorial term served as a transition linking her initial joint presidential period of wars of conquest to the next period. As US Secretary of State under President Obama she aggressively promoted global military supremacy.

Secretary of State Hillary Clinton: Naked Militarism Unleashed (2009 – 2013)
Whatever restraints Clinton faced as Senator dissolved as she ran amok during her term as Secretary of

State. Across Europe, Africa, Latin America and the Middle East, Hillary Clinton bombed, massacred and dispossessed millions of families, shredding entire societies and dismantling the institutions of organized civil life for scores of millions. She never balked at the prospect of ethnocide and even joked that NATO might become 'Al Qaeda's Air Force' as she pushed for a 'no-fly zone' over Syria.

Secretary Clinton promoted the terror mercenary brigades invading Syria in a bid to 'regime change' the secular government of al-Assad, driving several million Syrian refugees into flight. Entire ancient Syrian Christian communities were wiped out under her reign of 'regime change'.

Secretary Clinton directed US air force bombers and missiles to buttress the despotic Saudi monarchy's drive to obliterate Yemen.

Clinton unleashed the most savage bombing against Libya, destroying the country and leading to the ethnic cleansing of a million and a half Sub-Saharan workers and Black Libyans of sub-Saharan descent.

Clinton joked over the torture death of the wounded captive Libyan leader, Muammar Gadhafi, whose nauseating, almost pornographic murder by anal impalement was documented as a kind of 'regime-change' snuff film. Less known is the earlier, almost Old Testament-type slaughter of several of Gadhafi's non-political children and five small grandchildren by a deliberate US missile strike aimed at 'teaching the dictator' that even his smallest grandchild cannot be hidden.

Clinton, who bragged that her Biblical role model is (the ethnocidal) Queen Esther, has declared unconditional support for Israel's war crimes against Palestinians in Gaza, the West Bank and among the diaspora. Hillary endorsed and defended Israeli torture and prison camps for children, the elderly and the homeless.

Between 1999 and 2014, the Clinton Foundation received over $10 million from donors in Ukraine, which topped the list of donors for the period.[1] During Clinton's tenure as Secretary of State, the Viktor Pinchuk Foundation alone transferred at least $8.6 million to the Clinton charity between 2009 and 2013.[2] The Ukraine subsequently underwent regime change in 2013, promoted by Clinton protege Victoria Nuland and US NGOs such as the National Endowment for Democracy.

The forceful intervention by Russian President Vladimir Putin prevented Clinton's ethnic cleansing power grab in Crimea and the Donbass. The US retaliated by pushing for massive European Union economic sanctions against Russia.

Consistent with her pitiless Biblical role model, Clinton openly threatened to obliterate Iran with a nuclear war and incinerate 76 million Iranians to please her Uncle Netanyahu—a demented process that would poison a hundred million Arabs and perhaps a few million Israelis. Even the insane Israeli 'Samson option' was never dreamt of as being ordered from Washington, DC!

During her tenure as Secretary of State, Clinton actively obstructed any diplomatic moves to achieve a US-Iran agreement on nuclear technology, parroting the Israeli militarist solution against regional rivals!

Clinton has remained an unrepentant enemy to the emerging independent Latin American governments. In search of vassal states, Clinton promoted successful military coups in Honduras and Paraguay, but was defeated in Venezuela. She proudly touts the death squad regime in Honduras as among her foreign policy successes.

Hillary backed the death squad and narco-regimes in Colombia and Mexico, which killed over a hundred thousand civilians.

On the path to global war, Mme. Militarist has prepared to encircle Russia, stationing nuclear weapons in the Balkans and Poland. She promised that missiles would be placed in south central Europe and Ukraine.

Clinton raised the nuclear ante by hysterically claiming that the elected Russian President Vladimir Putin was 'worse than ISIS'... 'worse' than Hitler.

Repeatedly threatening global war and actually making aggressive regional wars should clearly have marked Hillary Clinton as unfit for the Presidency of the United States. She is politically, intellectually and emotionally unable to deal realistically with an independent Russia or any other independent power, including China and Iran. Her monomania is a course of violent regime changes, as she is unable to evaluate any of the catastrophes her policymaking has in fact already produced.

Hillary Clinton was the proud author and director of the so-called US 'pivot to Asia'. Clinton's 'pivot' has led to a massive buildup of the US air and naval forces surrounding China's maritime routes to its global markets and access to essential raw materials.

Clinton's hyper-militarism expanded US war zones to cover Australia, Japan and the Philippines, greatly heightening tensions and increasing the possibility of a military provocation leading to nuclear war with China.

No US presidential contender, past or present, has engaged in more offensive wars, in a shorter time, uttering greater nuclear threats than Hillary Clinton. That she has not yet set off the nuclear holocaust is probably a result of the Administrative constraints imposed on the Secretary of State by the less bloodthirsty President Obama. These limitations will end if and when Hillary Clinton is 'elected' president of the United States in a process that the electorate increasingly knows is 'rigged' toward that outcome.

Donald Trump: the Peaceful Road to Recession

In sharp contrast to the militarist Mme. Clinton, Donald Trump, 'the Businessman', has adopted a relatively peaceful approach to international politics for an American presidential candidate in the current era.

'Businessman' Trump envisions productive negotiations with Russian President Putin. Employing his loudly trumpeted deal-making genius to benefit the United States, Trump predicts economic and diplomatic successes with Russia, China, and other major powers.

Angered at US military allies enjoying decades of US Treasury largesse, as president, Trump promises to withdraw US military bases from Asia and Europe, and demand that overseas allies pony-up for their own defense.

What the war mongers in the mass media, academia and Washington bureaucracy, dismiss as 'Trump's isolationism', The Businessman describes as rebuilding America by converting overseas military spending into domestic infrastructure projects and 'real' jobs in America.

Trump's 'America First' policy, under his 'Make America Great Again' slogan, does not envision wars of conquest against Muslim countries, especially since these have already led to massive floods of Muslim refugees, threatening trade and stability, and to Trump opposition to the entry of more Muslim refugees into the US. Trump's foreign policy of limited military goals and warfare is diametrically opposed to Clinton's total war strategy. Trump, ridiculed by his rivals for 'his small hands', does not appear to have Hillary's itchy trigger finger on the nuclear button!

Trump mouths contradictory economic statements, especially his proposals to rebuild America, while operating in the framework of an imperial system. As President of the United States, his protectionist policies will come into direct confrontation with US and global 'finance and monopoly capitalism' and will likely lead to systematic disinvestment and a disastrous economic collapse or, more likely, the Businessman-President's capitulation to the status quo.

The problem is not Trump's pledges to tax the rich (as he occasionally promises), or expand Social Security (as he claims), but his failure to admit that these policies would lead to massive flight by the capitalist elite to avoid taxes. The major threat is that, if Trump follows-up on his America-First policies, there will be massive capital resistance and a Congressional revolt by both finance-dominated political parties, which will paralyze any hope for his economic agenda.

Without political independence to implement his domestic economic agenda, Trump will have to face a massive investment and lending revolt from capitalists and bankers who would be very willing to drive the fragile economy into a major recession, threatening a kind of domestic economic sabotage.

Trump's Republican Party (and certainly the Democrats as well) will never support a program which will force multinational capital to sacrifice its reliance on cheap overseas labor and double digit profits in order to create American jobs and employ American workers at living wages.

As President, Trump would not even secure a handful of Congressional votes to increase taxes on plutocrats to fund his proposed large-scale public works, infrastructure and job-creation projects.

The Businessman President would face the full fury of the powerful military-industrial-high tech complex if and when he attempted to retire US global military forces from Europe, Asia, the Middle East and Africa. Congress has already made its position clear, when the Pentagon in 2015 proposed such a move.

The non-politician Trump's historic rise to national political prominence has its roots in the ideas and values of the majority of working people who have been marginalized by the media moguls and Wall Street riff-raff. Today Trump's themes and ideas resonate with the mainstream of voters.

Several dominant ideas have circulated in his speeches and interviews.

First, Trump rejects 'globalization' (the watered-down PR term for imperialism) and 'free trade' (a euphemism for the transfer of profits extracted from US workers to business investment abroad). Trump's narrative resonates with the recent anti-Wall Street 'Occupy' movements opposing the power of 0.1% super rich against the vast majority.

Secondly, Trump embraces economic nationalism in his slogan "Make American Great Again".

The third theme that draws millions is Trump's notion that the US should reject the policy of serial 'regime change'. Too many American workers and their families resent having been exploited, maimed and slaughtered to serve multiple wars in the Middle East, Asia and Europe for the interests of US warlords, bankers, Zionists and other imperial royalties. Trump argues that the entire inflated security and corporate welfare system has led to an untenable debt payments spiral. He argues that we should not initiate and engage in perpetual overseas wars against Muslim countries as a way to avoid domestic attacks by individual terrorists. During an early foreign policy debate, Trump shocked the political establishment when he accused the Bush Administration of deliberately lying the country into the disastrous invasion of Iraq. This 'truth-telling' elicited wild applause from the mass Republican electorate.

Trump's goal is to strengthen American civilization and avoid provoking more 'clashes of civilizations'...

The fourth, and probably most attractive, message to most Americans is Trump's powerful assault on Washington and Wall Street elites, and their academic and media apologists.

Millions of Americans have been disgusted with the Bushes, the Clintons, and Obama, as well as with JPMorgan, Goldman Sachs, Hank Paulson *et al.*, whose policies have exacerbated class inequalities through multiple banking swindles and financial crashes, all bailed out by the American tax payers.

Fifth, Trump's loud, brash exposure of the mass media's lies and propaganda has resonated with the same deep distrust felt by the American public. His talent for talking directly and bluntly to the public and on the internet has led to his enormous appeal. He does not engage in conspiratorial thinking but acknowledges that the Edward Snowden revelations have unmasked the government's deceptions and its program of espionage against the people, destroying the foundations for democratic discourse.

Trump might win the election based on his 'five truths' and his pledge to 'make America great again', but more likely he will lose because he has insulted the traditional establishment, the Latinos, African Americans, feminists, trade union bureaucrats and their followers from both parties.

For the elites, if blocking Trump's domestic economic agenda requires a financial crash to defend globalization, serial wars and the 0.1%, then tighten your belts!

This November, the country will face the disagreeable choice between a proven nuclear warmonger and a captive of Wall Street. I will try to keep warm, roast chestnuts and avoid thinking about Mme. President's Looming Mushroom Cloud.

Endnotes

1   James V. Crimaldi and Rebecca Ballhaus, "Clinton Charity Tapped Foreign Friends," *Wall Street Journal*, March 19, 2015.

2   Ekaterina Blinova, "Clinton's Charity Ties With Oligarchs Behind Ukrainian Coup Revealed" < http://www.globalresearch.ca/clintons-charity-ties-with-oligarchs-behind-ukrainian-coup-revealed/5475866

| Chapter Two |

DEMOCRATIC PARTY PRIMARIES: "PROGRESSIVES" AS POLITICAL CONTRACEPTIVES

Introduction

Over the past few decades, insurgent mass movements reflecting political discontent with the domestic economy and imperialist foreign policy have emerged to challenge the leadership and policies of the Democratic Party (DP). There are good reasons for this: The Democratic Party in power in Congress and the White House presided over:
(1) the deepening of inequality between labor and capital;
(2) the decline of real wages;
(3) the approval of repressive legislation;
(4) the reduction of trade union membership by two-thirds;
(5) deepening inequality between the races;
(6) a trillion dollar (and counting) bailout of the banks and Wall Street;
(7) mortgage foreclosure against millions of home-owners;

(8) endless 'police state' abuses by federal and local police;
(9) deregulation of the financial system; and
(10) the off-shoring of manufacturing jobs and service employment.

Over the same period, the Democratic Party has supported wars and invasions against Indo-China, Panama, Grenada, Yugoslavia, Iraq, Afghanistan, Libya, Syria, Somalia and scores of clandestine military operations, including the recent and current proxy-wars in Georgia and Ukraine.

Popular movements emerged and mass public opinion expressed hostility toward both major parties. Hence, the third parties struck a responsive note among the electorate leading to the Democratic Party leadership feeling threatened by a possible defection by wage and salaried voters, especially to supporting Ralph Nader.

Yet in the end, nothing came of the discontent. Despite large-scale and deeply felt anger and popular outbursts of protests, including the million-strong street demonstrations against the invasion of Iraq in 2002-2003, the Democratic Party continued to dominate the 'progressive' electorate or relegated it to demoralized abstention.

This essay addresses the following questions:
(1) Why have mass movements and genuinely disaffected progressive voters and activists been unable to break with the Democratic Party, despite its consistently abominable record on foreign and domestic policy?
(2) How was the pro-Wall Street, pro-imperialist Democratic Party able to retain the support of an electorate, which overwhelmingly polls in favor of health care reform via a national, single-payer health plan, a living minimum wage, the end to police-state surveillance and against serial wars and invasions?

From Protest to Political Hostages

American mass movements have been successful in mobilizing hundreds of thousands in opposition to Washington's support of the South African apartheid regime, Central American dictators, wars in the Middle East and racist legislation. Progressives have educated and organized millions to oppose Wall Street and the Democratic Party's more recent bailout of banks.

Without fail, every time mass movements and the popular electorate have opted for independent social action outside of the Democratic Party, a 'dissident' politician has emerged from within the Party mouthing many of the criticisms and demands of the social movements and the critical electorate.

These Democrat 'dissidents' organize 'grass roots' campaigns in popular venues, soliciting small scale contributions and making promises to put an end to 'Big Money and Big Business' domination of the electoral process.

Such Democrat dissidents round up millions of votes and hundreds of delegates to the Democratic Convention and then ... they inevitably lose to the Party machine and meekly submit ... reasserting their loyalty to the 'greater good' of the Democrats against the 'greater evil' of the Republicans.

The radical rhetoric used during the campaign is consciously designed to obscure the dissidents' fundamental loyalty to the Democratic Party, its military machine, its billionaire fundraisers, and its Wall Street economic policy strategists.

The pre-ordained primary campaign defeat of the Democrat dissidents is not the real issue here: The essential political consequence is that the dissidents channel mass social disaffection back into the Democratic Party, thereby undermining any independent political initiative capable of breaking the duopoly stranglehold. In animal husbandry, they are like the handsome goat who tricks the flock into entering the big slaughter-pen of their social and political aspirations.

By endorsing the crowned Party nominee, these dissidents discredit the very critical ideas and social programs they claimed to promote. They demoralize and depoliticize important segments of the electorate. They demobilize and disorient the social activists who had worked for the social transformation promised by their campaign program.

Most important, by reorienting the peace and justice movements and the neighborhood and anti-racism community organizations into Democratic Party electoral politics, they empty the streets, neighborhoods, and workplaces of effective activists.

A brief survey of presidential campaigns over the past thirty-five years confirms this analysis.

Jesse Jackson and the Rainbow Hustle: 1984 and 1988

Jesse Jackson was an important leader-activist in the civil rights movement. Based in Chicago, he helped organize tens of thousands of African Americans and developed ties with other minorities, white progressives, and trade unions.

Jackson opposed President Reagan's assault on the trade unions, especially the firing of thousands of air controllers. Jackson's opposition to Apartheid South Africa and Reagan's invasion of Grenada and the escalation of military spending gained him credibility in the peace movement.

Millions looked to Jesse Jackson for political leadership and a new political direction. He negotiated with the bosses of the Democratic Party for his entry into the primaries. The deal was that he would compete with the traditional politicians, but immediately submit to the leadership if he lost the nomination.

Jackson mobilized hundreds of thousands of activists from the northern ghettos to the Ivy League college campuses and from the textile factories of North Carolina to the cotton fields of Mississippi. He rolled out the rhetoric about social justice, raising the minimum wage, a single payer (Medicare for All) national health plan, and a massive transfer of public funds from the Pentagon to domestic social programs.

He secured an impressive 18% of the vote in the 1984 Democratic primaries. Upon defeat, he immediately capitulated and endorsed the Wall Street Cold Warrior, Walter Mondale. He campaigned for Mondale with the promise that the Rainbow Coalition would influence the campaign and subsequent Mondale presidency. Nothing of the sort happened. Mondale lost. Reagan was re-elected. The 'rainbow coalition' was as ephemeral as its namesake.

Four years later, a recycled Jesse Jackson trotted out the same rhetoric, the grass roots organizing, the ghetto gab, the poverty hustle, and the pot of gold at the end of the rainbow coalition with white and black togetherness... to the amusement of the party bosses and corporate funders.

It was 'All hands on deck': The street movements shifted from concrete local struggles to door-to-door voter registration for the Democrats. Trade union locals were attracted to Jackson's 'save American jobs' rhetoric. Middle class progressives were attracted to Jackson's promise to cut the military budget.

Jackson received a substantial 29% of the Democratic primary vote. Michael Dukakis won the nomination and, as promised, Jesse Jackson endorsed the party's choice and instructed all the civil rights, social justice, and peace activists and anti-Wall Streeters to work for his election.

Dukakis was resoundingly defeated by George Bush Sr. in the 1988 election.

At the end of the 'rainbow' and over a demoralized and de-politicized peace movement, the Bush Administration led the US into the First Gulf War. The wreckage from the popular movements-turned-electoral machines offered little resistance.

Confused by Jackson's double discourse, the disaffected masses fractured. Four years later, the few pieces were picked up by Wall Street flunky "Bill" Clinton. Once in office and after tooting his victorious saxophone, President 'Slick Willy' proceeded to decimate welfare programs, roll back the Glass-Steagall Act to deregulate the banks, launch a merciless ninety-day war to break up Yugoslavia, and maintain ten years of bombs and starvation sanctions against Iraq—causing the deaths of 500,000 children and many more adults.

Cowboy Dennis Kucinich and the 2004 Primaries: Keeping Progressive Livestock in the Democratic Party Corral

Just when disgust at the consequences of Clinton's rotten policies and peccadilloes and George Bush, Jr's grotesque wars were beginning to unite the disaffected, Dennis Kucinich popped up from nowhere to launch a white working class version of the Jesse Jackson Rainbow Coalition in the Democratic Party primaries of 2004. Saving a lot of money on placards, he re-cycled the same slogans about a national health system, minimum wage boost, higher taxes for the rich, anti-Wall Street rhetoric, and public ownership of utilities used by the Jacksonites.

Since there was still a substantial, strong anti-war movement, he called for the impeachment of President Bush (Jr.) for lying to the American people about Iraq. He criticized Congressional Democrats for supporting the fabricated pretexts to invade Iraq and called for the withdrawal of US troops from the Middle East.

His presidential primary campaign within the Democratic Party attracted a small army of disaffected voters and contributors who otherwise would have bolted from the party for the Greens and their candidate, Ralph Nader. In the Democratic Party Convention, Dennis (looking more like 'Alfred E. Newman' than any righteous working class leader) petered out with nary a mumble. He lost the nomination to the Uber-militarist and upper class hero, John Kerry, without even a floor-fight or speech. He endorsed the obnoxious crown prince of the Democratic bosses, Kerry, an ardent pro-war, member of the billionaire class, and defender of the US Constitution-shredding Patriot Act.

Kucinich managed to corral the anti-war and anti-Wall Street Democrats into submission, seriously undermining the anti-Bush mass movements, especially the anti-war activists, and the rising tide of Americans who openly favored the Single Payer National Health program, an extension of Medicare for All.

Kucinich ran again in 2008 but he was already damaged goods. His 'belly crawl' performance at the 2004 Democratic Convention had alienated most of his backers. But even more important in relegating Dennis to the dustbin was the emergence of a new, slicker, and infinitely more persuasive con-man: Barack Obama, the Hawaii-raised, Ivy-league polished, and Chicago-crowned chameleon of many colors, cadences and clichés, who burst on the scene playing every instrument in the band!

Barack Obama: The Ultimate Progressive Rabble Rouser and Master of Deceit

Barack Obama's con-job far surpassed any previous

effort by Jackson or Kucinich. His mind-boggling ascension on rhetorical bubbles left rival Hillary Clinton, long used to the cant of 'Slick Willie', literally pop-eyed and slack jawed. During the 2008 primary he embraced the progressive demands of the anti-war movement, promising to end the Iraq war, bring home the troops from Afghanistan and close the US torture camp at Guantanamo Bay. He promised to finally develop a national health plan (hinting broadly at a Medicare-for-All model) and regulate Wall Street's unbridled swindles and speculation.

Easily seeing through his fluffy rhetoric, the Democratic Party's Wall Street backers secured hundreds of millions from billionaires with which to finance a real grass roots movement in style, defeating an astonished Hillary Clinton in the Democratic primaries and swamping the mega-millionaire Republican candidate, 'Mitt' Romney, in the general election.

The Zelig-like Obama adopted the Baptist minister's deep and musical cadences in front of black audiences while savaging and disowning his militant black religious mentor from his Chicago 'community-organizing' day, the Reverend Jeremiah Wright, who had condemned the war in Iraq in frank Biblical terms and alienated his Chicago Zionist financial backers and Israel-centric inner council. No longer useful, the good Reverend was effectively thrown under the bus—an object lesson on introducing Ivy League graduates into mass community struggles and enabling their ambitions.

In office, Obama allocated a trillion dollars to bailout Wall Street while letting two million American householders sink under mortgage debt and foreclosures.

He expanded ongoing wars in Afghanistan and Iraq and went on to launch new wars in Libya, Syria, and Yemen. He supported the violent coups against popularly elected governments (regime changes) in Honduras, Ukraine and Egypt.

The re-cycled and bamboozled anti-war leaders, who backed his candidacy and lies, were discredited, and the remaining "movement" fractured.

Initially upward of 80% of US public opinion expressed support for the anti-Wall Street 'Occupy Movement' but they had no mass-based political organization to sustain the struggle after many of their leaders swam and ultimately sank, tied to the lies of Obama.

Under Obama more American blacks have been murdered by police with complete impunity; more abortion providers assassinated and clinics bombed than under any white Republican president. As for 'humanitarian intervention': In Libya, tens of thousands, including ethnic sub-Saharan Africans (contract workers and Libyan citizens), died in the post-Gadhafi ethnic cleansing of Libya by the racist warlords unleashed by Obama's air assault.

The bewitched progressives were befuddled by the Ivy League's black president and didn't notice that social inequalities had deepened at an alarming rate. As for access to health care, the American people were forced to buy private insurance plans (many of which were worthless), while deductibles and co-pays skyrocketed, forcing all but the well-salaried to forego necessary medical care. The notion that 'access to health insurance' was equivalent to having effective health care has been one of the biggest shams of the Obama era: Life expectancy for large segments of the low income rural and small town Americans has dropped—an unimaginable development in previous eras.

During Obama's presidency, the political climate turned rabidly to the right and the progressives turned tail and ran. Right wing extremists swept the Republican Party and then seized control of the Congress and the Senate.

After seven years of failures, frustration and futility under Obama, progressives found themselves without a movement or prospects. Over 92% of US private sector workers were unorganized and faced continued decline in their standard of living. Black, Chicano, and Asian neighborhoods were subject to large-scale, brutal police raids, and the extra-judicial killing of minority youth, the homeless, mentally ill, and the poor continued with impunity. Over two million immigrant workers were incarcerated and expelled. Tens of thousands of young immigrant and refugee mothers and their children were held in private prison camps.

The Republicans promised to extend Obama's reactionary agenda without the smiling blackface mask. They assured greater tax handouts to Wall Street, with none of the embarrassing rhetorical flourishes, and more wars, without the sanctimonious 'humanitarian' cant.

Against this expanding panorama of social deterioration and war-weariness, (a backdrop, which would normally open up the possibility for alternative politics...), Bernie appeared. Bernie Sanders was to incarnate the Fourth Coming of the progressive Democratic primary campaigner-messiah and scupper any real movement to the left.

Bernie Sanders: After the Black Con-Artist, Bring out the Jewish House Radical!

By 2015, US society was deeply polarized. After seven years of Wall Street pillage, under Democratic President Obama, the mass of working people were looking for an alternative. On the horizon there was only more of the same promised from the rabid right which ran the Republican Party. Massive voter abstention had propelled the Republicans to power in both Houses in the elections of 2010, 2012, and 2014. Terror-mongering, the so-called "Global War on

Terror", no longer cut any ice with a population terrified of losing their miserable jobs or being bankrupted by an illness in the family. The Pentagon resorted to paying unemployed actors to stage 'spontaneous' displays of patriotism at huge sporting events—dressed up as veterans and running about on the fields with huge flags. There has been a big drop in healthy, young Americans willing to sign up and fight in overseas wars despite the continued prospect of being mired in poverty-wage jobs in what is billed as the recovered domestic economy. Nor were the mass of disaffected working people flocking to the Democratic Party's plutocrat-of-choice, Hillary Clinton, the warmonger, Wall Street favorite and pro-Israel candidate par excellence. The stage was set for mass voter abstention and a resounding electoral defeat for a deflated Democratic Party by a disgusted electorate. As a presidential candidate Hillary would have to fight tooth and nail to meet the challenge of even the most marginal lunatic candidate from the increasingly bizarre Republican Party—because the Democrats' disaffected voter base would stay home.

Behold! A raspy rabble rouser, a 'democratic socialist', floated in on a cloud of self-righteousness, conjuring up the illusion of a movement with promises of 'profound (and even profounder) changes'.

Like Jackson and Kucinich before him, Sanders launched right into The Rant: Against Wall Street, for a National Health Plan and a reduction of military spending (but not too much...). He added a few new planks about cancelling student debt, lowering tuition, ending the cap on the social security tax, and greater regulation of Wall Street.

Early polls gave Sanders 25% of the Democratic preferences.

Bernie assured his worried Democratic Party handlers that should Clinton win the primaries, Bernie (and his followers) would immediately and unconditionally support the Party's warmongering, Wall Street candidate of choice.

What are we to make of his promises and his radical program, if after putting forward a comparatively principled stand, he can easily make a 180 degree turn to support the most discredited dregs of the Democratic Party—those largely responsible for the country's social and economic decline?

Conclusion

The whole history of Democratic Party 'progressives' has been one of deceit, hypocrisy, and betrayal of millions of workers, minorities and other oppressed and excluded groups.

They rant and rave, till the votes are counted and then they dissolve their electoral organization and push their supporters into the Party electoral campaign!

They do not continue the struggle outside of the corrupt party—they simply go belly up, 'graciously conceding defeat' and wagging their tails, hoping for a reward (like some inconsequential, toothless position within the administration) if the Democrats win.

After every one of the radicals' defeats, their supporters are left adrift. Indeed, they are worse off than before, because their movements have been diverted into the Democratic primaries and away from the needs of the communities. The historical record is clear: After Jesse Jackson lost, the Rainbow Coalition fell apart; civil rights movements were weakened; police violence against blacks continued and even worsened.

After Kucinich ran and lost, his grassroots supporters within the trade unions had no mechanism to block the relocation of auto, steel, and textile plants overseas.

After Obama conned progressive Americans, the peace and justice movement virtually disappeared. The church, trade union, neighborhood alliances who celebrated Barack Obama's 'historic victory' have in reality experienced historical retreats. The only things "historic" about Obama's terms in office have been (1) the trillion dollar bailout of Wall Street, (2) the number of simultaneous wars waged by the Pentagon, (3) the millions of people of color slaughtered in Libya, Syria, and Yemen (4) the thousands of minorities killed in cities, big and small of the USA (5) and the tens of thousands lost to premature deaths in economically devastated rural and small town America.

The current "Bernie" Sanders roadshow is just recycling the past, right down to the same rhetorical and inconsequential promises of his predecessors.

Some of his gullible followers claim that he is important for "raising issues" when in fact he will just raise them only to then demoralize their advocates.

Other pundits claim he is 'challenging the Democratic Party from the left' when in fact his candidacy is doing everything possible to prevent millions of disaffected ex-Democratic voters, mostly workers and minorities, from rejecting the Democrats and joining or forming alternative political movements.

The key to understanding why millions of Americans, fed up with 30 years of declining living and health standards, deepening inequalities and perpetual wars, do not form an alternative party is that they have been repeatedly conned and corralled in the Democratic Party by the house radicals.

Jackson, Kucinich, Obama and Sanders promised radical changes in the primaries and then went gone on to hand their supporters, mostly disaffected workers, over to the Party oligarchs, abandoning them after having drained and diverted their past social movements and jettisoned their future hopes like cast-off condoms. Is there any wonder why so many abstain!

| Chapter Three |

PRESIDENTIAL ELECTIONS 2016: THE REVOLT OF THE MASSES

Introduction

The presidential elections of 2016 have several unique characteristics that defy common wisdom about political practices in 21st century America.

Clearly the established political machinery—party elites and their corporate backers—have (in part) lost control of the nomination process and confront unwanted candidates who are campaigning with programs and pronouncements that polarize the electorate.

But there are other more specific factors, which have energized the electorate and speak to recent US history. These portend and reflect a realignment of US politics.

In this essay, we will outline these changes and their larger consequences for the future of American politics and examine how these factors affect each of the two major parties.

Democratic Party Politics: The Context of Realignment

The rise and decline of President Obama has seriously

dented the appeal of 'identity politics'—the idea that ethnic, race and gender-rooted identities can modify the power of finance capital (Wall Street), the militarists, the Zionists, and police-state officials. Clearly, manifest voter disenchantment with identity politics has opened the door for class politics of a specific kind.

Candidate Bernie Sanders appeals directly to the class interests of workers and salaried employees. But the class issue arises within the context of an electoral polarization and, as such, it does not reflect a true class polarization, or rising class struggle in the streets, factories or offices.

In fact, the electoral class polarization is a reflection of the recent major trade union defeats in Michigan, Wisconsin, and Ohio. The trade union confederation (AFL-CIO) has almost disappeared as a social and political factor, representing only 7% of private sector workers. Working class voters are well aware that top trade union leaders, who receive an average of $500,000-a-year in salaries and benefits, are deeply ensconced in the Democratic Party elite. While individual workers and local unions are active supporters of the Sanders campaign, they do so as members of an amorphous multi-class electoral movement and not as a unified 'workers bloc'.

The Sanders electoral movement has not grown out of a national social movement. The peace movement is virtually moribund; the civil rights movements are weak, fragmented, and localized; the Black Lives Matter movement has peaked and declined while the Occupy Wall Street movement is a distant memory.

In other words, these recent movements, at best, provide some activists and some impetus for the Sanders electoral campaign. Their presence highlights a few of the issues that the Sanders electoral movement promotes in its campaign.

In fact, the Sanders electoral movement does not grow out of existing, ongoing mass movements as much as it fills the political vacuum resulting from their demise. The electoral insurgency reflects the defeats of trade union officials allied with incumbent Democratic politicians as well as the limitation of the 'direct action' tactics of the Black Lives Matter and Occupy movements.

Since the Sanders electoral movement does not directly and immediately challenge capitalist profits and public budget allocations, it has not been subject to state repression. Repressive authorities calculate that this 'buzz' of electoral activity will last only a few months and then recede into the Democratic Party or voter apathy. Moreover, they are constrained by the fact that tens of millions of Sanders supporters are involved in all the states and not concentrated in any region.

The Sanders electoral movement aggregates hundreds of thousands of micro-local struggles and allows expression of the disaffection of millions with class grievances, at no risk or cost (as in loss of jobs or police repression) to the participants. This is in stark contrast to repression at the workplace or in the urban streets.

The electoral polarization reflects horizontal (class) and vertical (intra-capitalist) social polarizations.

Below the elite 10% and especially among the young middle class, political polarization favors the Sanders electoral movement. Trade union bosses, the Black Congressional Caucus members and the Latino establishment all embrace the anointed choice of the political elite of the Democratic Party: Hillary Clinton. Whereas, young Latinos, working women, and rank and file trade unionists support the insurgent electoral movement. Significant sectors of the African American population, who have failed to advance (and have actually regressed) under Democratic President

Obama or have seen police repression expand under the 'First Black President', are turning to the insurgent Sanders campaign. Millions of Latinos, disenchanted with their leaders, who are tied to the Democratic elite and have done nothing to prevent the massive deportations under Obama, are a potential base of support for 'Bernie'.

However, the most dynamic social sector in the Sanders electoral movement are students, who are excited by his program of free higher education and the end of post-graduation debt peonage.

The malaise of these sectors finds its expression in the 'respectable revolt of the middle class': a voters' rebellion, which has temporarily shifted the axis of political debate within the Democratic Party to the left.

The Sanders electoral movement raises fundamental issues of class inequality and racial injustice in the legal, police and economic system. It highlights the oligarchical nature of the political system—even as the Sanders-led movement attempts to use the rules of the system against its owners. These attempts have not been very successful within the Democratic Party apparatus, where the Party bosses have already allocated hundreds of non-elected, so-called 'mega-delegates' to Clinton, despite Sander's successes in the early primaries.

The very strength of the electoral movement has a strategic weakness: it is in the nature of electoral movements to coalesce for elections and to dissolve after the vote.

The Sanders leadership has now indicated that it regards itself as building a national social movement that can continue the class and social struggles during and after the election. But in fact, if Sanders maintains his pledge to support the established leadership of the Democratic Party if he loses the nomination to Clinton, this will lead to a profound disillusionment of his supporters and breakup of his projected movement, which has accepted his movement leadership primarily because he offers the best available *electoral* option.

Trump and Revolt on the Right

The Trump electoral campaign has many of the features of a Latin American nationalist-populist movement. Like the Argentine Peronist movement, it combines protectionist, nationalist economic measures that appeal to small and medium size manufacturers and displaced industrial workers with populist right-wing 'great nation chauvinism'.

This is reflected in Trump's attacks on globalization, a proxy for Peronist anti-imperialism.

Trump's attack on the Muslim minority in the US is a thinly veiled embrace of right wing clerical fascism.

Where Peron campaigned against financial oligarchies and the invasion of foreign ideologies, Trump scorns the elites and denounces the 'invasion' of Mexican immigrants.

Trump's appeal is rooted in the deep amorphous anger of the downwardly mobile middle class, which has no ideology ... but plenty of resentment at its declining status, crumbling stability, and drug-afflicted families (witness the overtly expressed concerns of white voters in the recent New Hampshire primary).

Trump projects personal power to workers who bridle under impotent trade unions, disorganized civic groups, and marginalized local business associations, all unable to counter the pillage, power and large-scale corruption of the financial swindlers who rotate between Washington and Wall Street with total impunity.

These populist classes get vicarious thrills from the spectacle of Trump snapping and slapping career politicians and economic elites alike, even as he parades his capitalist success.

They prize his symbolic defiance of the political elite as he flaunts his own capitalist elite credentials.

For many of his suburban backers he is the Great Moralizer, who in his excess zeal, occasionally, commits pardonable gaffes out of zealous exuberance—a crude Oliver Cromwell for the 21st century.

Indeed, there also may be a less overt ethno-religious appeal to Trump's campaign: his white-Anglo-Saxon Protestant identity appeals to these same voters in the face of their apparent marginalization. These 'Trumpistas' are not blind to the fact that not a single WASP judge sits on the Supreme Court and there are few, if any, WASPs among the top economic officials in Treasury, Commerce, or the Fed (Lew, Fischer, Yellen, Greenspan, Bernancke, Cohen, Pritzker, etc.). As Trump is not up-front about his identity, it eases his voter appeal.

WASP voters quietly resent the Wall Street bailouts and the perceived privileged position of Catholics, Jews, and African-Americans in the Obama Administration. Trump's direct, public condemnation of President Bush for deliberately misleading the nation into invading Iraq (and the implication of treason), has been a big plus.

Trump's nationalist-populist appeal is matched by his bellicose militarism and thuggish authoritarianism. His public embrace of torture and police state controls (to 'fight terrorism') appeals to the pro-military right. On the other hand, his friendly overtures to Russian President Putin ('one tough guy willing to face another') and his support to end the Cuban embargo appeals to trade-minded business elites. His calls to withdraw US troops from Europe and Asia appeals to fortress America voters, while his calls to carpet bomb ISIS appeals to the nuclear extremists. Interestingly,

Trump's support for Social Security and Medicare, as well as his call for medical coverage for the indigent and his open acknowledgement of Planned Parenthood's vital services to poor women, appeals to older citizens, compassionate conservatives and independents.

Trump offers a left-right amalgam: Protectionist and pro-business appeals, anti-Wall Street and pro-industrial capitalism proposals, defense of US workers and attacks on Latino workers and Muslim immigrants. This has broken the traditional boundaries between popular and right wing politics of the Republican Party.

Trumpism is not a coherent ideology, but a volatile mix of improvised positions, adapted to appeal to marginalized workers, resentful middle classes (marginalized WASPs), and, above all, to those who feel unrepresented by Wall Street Republicans and liberal Democratic politicians based on identity politics (Black, Hispanic, women and Jews).

Trump's movement is based on a cult of the personality: it has enormous capacity to convoke mass meetings without mass organization or a coherent social ideology.

Its fundamental strength is its spontaneity, novelty, and hostile focus on strategic elites. Its strategic weakness is the lack of an organization that can be sustained after the electoral process. There are few Trumpista cadres and militants among his adoring fans. If Trump loses (or is cheated out of the nomination by a 'unity' candidate trotted out by the Party elite) his organization will dissipate and fragment. If Trump wins the Republican nomination he will draw support from Wall Street, especially if faced with a Sanders Democratic candidacy. If he wins the general election and becomes president, he will seek to strengthen executive power and move toward a 'Bonapartist' presidency.

Conclusion

The rise of a social democratic movement within the Democratic Party and the rise of a *sui generis* nationalist-populist rightist movement in the Republican Party reflect the fragmented electorate and deep vertical and horizontal fissures characterizing the US ethno-class structure. Commentators grossly oversimplify when they reduce the revolt to incoherent expressions of anger.

The shattering of the established elite's control is a product of deeply experienced class and ethnic resentments, of formerly privileged groups experiencing declining mobility, of local businesspeople experiencing bankruptcy due to globalization (imperialism), and of citizens' resentment at the power of finance capital (the banks) and its overwhelming control of Washington.

The electoral revolts on the left and right may dissipate but they will have planted the seeds of a democratic transformation or of a nationalist-reactionary revival.

| Chapter Four |

TRUMP "THE FASCIST": BACKDOOR BACKING OF POLITICAL PSYCOPATH HILLARY CLINTON

Introduction

From left to right a raucous chorus has emerged to denounce Republican Presidential primary frontrunner Donald Trump as a 'fascist'. They cite his campaign promises to build an Israeli-style wall along the US border, his threats to expel eleven million undocumented immigrants, and to restrict foreign Muslims from entering the US, as well as the way his pugnacious face and arm resemble those of Benito Mussolini ('he juts out his chin, he raises his arm'). They decry his extreme nationalism as 'resembling Hitler's policy', by which they mean his opposition to detrimental free trade agreements and his slogan to "Make America Great... Again."

In this chapter I will critically compare the current cartoonish image of fascism with fascism's historical reality, and then analyze the so-called "lesser evil" politics behind the re-invention of an American fascist in the guise of billionaire Donald Trump.

Fascism: Fact and Fiction

Historically, fascist politics involved organized mass movements, armed militia, and paramilitary groups who assaulted political opponents, violently censored critical speech, and suppressed the right to assemble. Fascists scapegoated minorities, especially gypsies and Jews, and burned trade unions and leftist headquarters, assassinating their leaders and beating their members. Programmatically, they attacked pacifists and defended overseas wars and empires in the name of 'living space'. Evoking a past imperial glory, they were not isolationists.

Candidate Trump has not organized anything resembling a mass movement, let alone an armed militia. There are no 'Trumpeting Brown Shirts'. At most, the police and a handful of his (often elderly) white supporters have punched a few KKK-dressed provocateurs who have physically disrupted and threatened Trump's public meetings and his exercise of free speech. In fact, the 'fascist' disruption of democratic freedoms seems to be mostly organized and practiced by his political rivals.

Trump, far from scapegoating the powerful Jewish minority in this country, gave a shamelessly Israel-centric speech and received a standing ovation from nearly 18,000 mostly prominent Jews at the March 2016 meeting of the major pro-Israel lobby, AIPAC.

His rhetoric, concerning the expulsion of 11 million undocumented workers from Mexico and Central America and the building of a border wall, is a far cry from the actual practice of imprisoning and violently expelling over two million undocumented Latinos, as has taken place under the Clinton-Bush-Obama/Clinton regimes. At worst, Trump promises to continue the existing federal policy on immigration and not create a 'fascist' rupture with past administrations. Is a rhetorical cement wall worse than the real wall of armed border police, helicopters and armed carriers that have operated under the presidencies of Clinton-Bush-Obama/Clinton with their hundreds of migrant deaths in the desert? Are declarations of a repressive immigration policy more 'fascist' coming from Trump's loud mouth than the actual official practice of violently seizing undocumented workers from their homes and workplaces leading to their long-term imprisonment and/or expulsion? Than expelling youth, raised and educated in this country, or violently splitting up productive, well-integrated families and imprisoning their main breadwinners for lack of documents? Because that's the official policy of the current and past three administrations.

There is far less of the truly fascist embrace of pre-emptive war and invasion in Trump's speeches than in the actual policies pursued by the Clinton-Bush-Obama/Clinton regimes. In fact, among Trump's numerous critics, especially his Republican rivals and the Hillary Clinton camp, we hear the loudest denunciations of his non-interventionist foreign policy (isolationism), which is "out of line" with the interventionist, overseas wars of current and past Republican and Democratic administrations. Trump's critics and media pundits are 'horror-struck' at his apparent willingness to co-operate with Russian President Putin against common enemies, such as ISIS. Is his pragmatic regard of Russia more or less fascist than his rivals' support for the Ukrainian putsch, orchestrated by the Obama regime in alliance with bona fide armed anti-Semitic Ukrainian fascists? His calls to dump NATO as an expensive drain on US treasure and manpower have the elite howling in outrage!

The propagandists, who paint Trump as a modern American fascist, cite his crude sexist remarks as 'examples of a misogynist totalitarian' while pointing favorably to Democratic candidate Hillary Clinton as potentially the 'first feminist President'. In regard to his alleged misogyny, the Donald pointed to Madame First Lady, Senator and Secretary Clinton's promotion of and critical role in US wars against Libya, Iraq and Syria where well over one million women have been rendered refugees, raped, injured or killed. Which is worse, one may ask: Crude locker room jokes or millions of orphaned boys and girls denied parents, homes, education and any future in the Middle East and North Africa? That is the world Midwife Hillary Clinton had helped to deliver.

Misogyny is in the eye of the deceiver.

Are Trump's verbal attacks on the practice of US multi-nationals relocating abroad to avoid US taxes and Wall Street financial houses hiding billions of the US elites' obscene wealth in offshore tax shelters, more detrimental to 'American values' (as charged) than Hillary Clinton's pandering to Wall Street while pocketing over $300,000 for each 45 minute sycophantic performance (marketed as her 'policy lectures'), or her decades of actively promoting globalization, including the US job-destroying NAFTA?

Clearly Trump currently lacks the program, organization and practice that define a fascist politician. At the very worst, he parrots the general line of attack against immigrants and Muslims. So far, he would just bar them from the US but not bomb them 'back to the stone-age'. This should be contrasted with the actual policies carried out by the war-criminals Clinton-Bush-Obama/Clinton. It would be hard for the Donald to 'trump' Hillary who threatened to 'obliterate Iran' and its scores of millions of citizens because of Iran's fictitious 'nuclear program'.

On the other hand, Trump's own meetings and rallies have been the victim of repeated disruption by organized groups acting like fascist thugs. We are witness to a role reversal in real life: Trump, the target of rabid sustained mass media attacks, is pronounced the fascist ...

Bashing Trump: Backdoor Backing of Hillary the Militarist Psychopath

If the objective case for labeling Trump a fascist is weak or non-existent, why do so many prestigious academics and journalists who understand the above-mentioned distinctions play this stupid game of calling him one?

The common sense explanation of their ruffled bluster is because they are setting up 'Trump-the- Straw-Dragon' in order to promote the poisonous Secretary Hillary Clinton as the 'lesser evil candidate' for President of the United States.

No serious observer minimally aware of Clinton's carnal embrace of multiple simultaneous disastrous and destructive wars in Ukraine, Iraq, Afghanistan, Yemen, Syria and Libya, could possibly support her—unless if they are convinced that a greater danger looms on the horizon and that "we have to defeat fascist Trump at all cost"? No serious democrat or wage and salaried employee can ignore Clinton's role as Wall Street's most shameless pimp unless they believe that a loud-mouth New York 'fascist' is worse than Wall Street.

The phony scaremongering about Trump's fascism just serves to cover up Clinton's most servile promotion of traitorous wars for the benefit of Israel. One should envision the thousands of desperate Syrian refugees clinging to decrepit boats in the Mediterranean when reading excerpts of Clinton's private e-mails: According to WikiLeaks, Hillary declared that:

> the best way to help Israel deal with Iran's growing nuclear capability [sic] is to help [sic] the people of Syria overthrow the regime of Bashar Assad ... The fall of the House of Assad could well ignite a sectarian war

between the Shiites and the majority Sunnis of the region drawing in Iran, which, *in the view of Israeli commanders* [italics added] would not be a bad thing for Israel and its Western allies.

Not a bad thing for Israel—but a cruel and criminal policy against a sovereign nation and multi-ethnic society. Clinton then followed through with these demented pronouncements, which can only be viewed as genocidal! Clinton promoted the most violent proxy war, uprooting over half of the civilian population of Syria and killing hundreds of thousands, while shredding a sovereign nation. Such was the extent of her pandering to her Israeli mentors and Plutocratic-Zionist funders.

To justify backing a serial warmonger, a US Secretary of State who has served Israel's interests, and a politician who has ditched her 'feminist principles' to collude with Wall Street billionaires, Hillary Clinton's smarmy supporters have had to invent an opponent who is even worse: creating and then denouncing "Trump the Fascist" serves as a backdoor justification for supporting a proven political psychopath!

| Chapter Five |

PLUTOCRATIC ZIONIST SUPPORT FOR HILLARY CLINTON

Introduction

Plutocratic Zionism is the three-way marriage of plutocracy, right wing Zionism, and US presidential candidate Hillary Clinton, a serial war criminal, racist and servant of Wall Street. How did this deadly ménage-a-trois come about? The answer is that a stratospherically wealthy donor group, dedicated to promoting Israel's dominance in the Middle East and deepening US military intervention in the region, has secured Clinton's unconditional support for Tel Aviv's ambitions and, in exchange, Hillary receives scores of millions to finance her Democratic Party foot soldiers and voters for her campaign.

Plutocratic Zionism and Clinton

Plutocratic Zionists are the leading financial backers of Clinton. Her million-dollar backers, among the most powerful financiers and media moguls in America, include: George Soros ($6 million), Marc Benioff, Roger Altman,

Steven Spielberg, Haim and Cheryl Saban ($3 million and counting), Jeffrey Katzenberg, Donald Sussman, Herb Sandler, Jay and Mark Pritzker, S. Daniel Abraham ($1 million), Bernard Schwartz, Marc Lasry, Paul Singer, David Geffen, Fred Eychaner, Norman Braman and Bernie Marcus. Waiting in the wings are the Koch brothers as well as the 'liberal' multi-billionaire, Michael Bloomberg who had contributed $11 million in 2012 elections. These erstwhile Republican funders are increasingly frightened by the anti-free trade and anti-intervention rhetoric of their party's front-runner, Donald Trump, and are approaching the solidly pro-Israel, pro-war and pro-Wall Street candidate, Madame Clinton.

Israel-First Ideologues and Clinton

In addition to the powerful Plutocratic Zionists, a vast army of Israel-First ideologues is behind Clinton, including 'veteran' arm-chair warmongers like Victoria Nuland Kagan, Donald and Robert Kagan, Robert Zoellick, Michael Chertoff, and Dov Zakheim, among so many other promoters of Washington's continuous wars on many fronts. Ms. Nuland-Kagan, as US Undersecretary of State for European and Eurasian Affairs, openly bragged about using hundreds of millions of dollars of US taxpayer money to finance the right-wing Ukrainian coup. Michael Chertoff, as head of Homeland Security after 9/11, jailed thousands of innocent Muslims while freeing five Israeli-Mossad agents arrested by the FBI for suspected involvement or pre-knowledge of the attacks in New York after they were seen filming the collapse of the towers and celebrating the event from a warehouse rooftop in New Jersey!

Plutocratic Zionists and the Israel-First ideologues support Ms. Clinton as a reward for her extraordinary military and economic activities on behalf of Tel Aviv's quest for regional dominance. Her accomplishments for the Jewish State include the promotion of full-scale wars, which have destroyed Iraq, Syria, Libya and Afghanistan; economic sanctions and blockade against Iran (she threatened to 'obliterate Iran' in 2007); and her own repeatedly stated unconditional support for Israel's devastation against the people imprisoned in Gaza, which has cost thousands of civilian lives and rendered hundreds of thousands homeless. (In a letter to her 'banker', Haim Saban, Hillary stated: "Israel didn't teach Hamas [the people of Gaza] a harsh enough lesson last year").

Clinton versus Trump: Moderation is in the Eyes of the Deceiver

The Plutocratic Zionists, Israel-First ideologues, the US mass media and their acolytes on Wall Street and the Republican and Democratic Party elite are all on a rampage against the wildly popular Republican frontrunner, Donald Trump, labeling him as 'a danger to everything America stands for.' Apart from savaging his persona, the anti-Trump chorus contrast his extremism with warmonger Clinton's pragmatism. A careful examination of the facts reveals who is the ultra-extremist and who deals with reality:

Women
Madame Clinton's much touted wars against the people of Iraq, Afghanistan, Syria and Libya have killed and maimed hundreds of thousands of women and children and uprooted millions of households. This bloody and undeniable record of mayhem was cited by Donald Trump when he argued that his policies would be much better for women than the Feminist Clinton's had been.

So far, Trump's worst offenses against women are his crude rhetorical misogynist quips, which pale before Hillary's bloody record of devastation.

African Americans
Clinton is backed by the leading black politicians who have long fed out of the Democratic Party patronage trough while selling the Clintons to the black electorate as ardent protectors of civil rights. In fact, as Steve Lendman has written, Hillary had referred to marginalized black youth as "super predators (with) no conscience, no empathy". During her husband Bill's presidency, she was on record supporting his draconian 'three strikes' crime laws, leading to the mass incarceration of hundreds of thousands of young blacks; and she backed his 'welfare reform' program, which shredded the social safety net for the poor and forced millions of impoverished mothers to work for sub-poverty wages, further eroding the stability of black female-headed households. On the African front, 'Sister' Secretary of State Hillary's war on Libya led to the displacement, rape, and murder of tens of thousands of black women of sub-Saharan origin at the hands of her jihadi warlord allies. Millions of black sub-Saharan migrants had lived and worked in Gadhafi's Libya for years, tens of thousands becoming Libyan citizens. They endured the horror of rampant ethnic cleansing in Clinton's 'liberated' Libya.

Trump, at worst, has done nothing of direct harm to African Americans and remains an enigma on black issues. He opposes Clinton's war on Libya and has vividly blamed her policies as responsible for the chaos and human misery in post-NATO bombing Libya.

Latinos
Under the Obama-Clinton administration almost

2 million Latino immigrants have been seized from their homes and workplaces, separated from their families and summarily expelled. As Secretary of State, Clinton backed the Honduran military coup that overthrew the elected government of President Zelaya and led directly to assassination of over three hundred activists, including feminist, indigenous, human rights and environmental leaders, like Berta Caceres. Clinton actively backed unsuccessful coups against the democratically elected Bolivian and Venezuelan governments.

Trump has verbally threated to extend and deepen the Obama-Clinton expulsion of whatever remains of the estimated 11 million undocumented immigrant Latino workers after Obama's expulsion of the 2 million and the hundreds of thousands who have voluntarily gone home. His 'extremist' vision is completely in line with that of his allegedly 'pragmatic' opponent whose State Department promoted the destruction of so many Latino families in the US.

Foreign Policy

Clinton has launched or promoted more simultaneous wars than any Secretary of State in US history. She was the leading force behind the US bombing of Libya and the brutal regime change that has fractured that nation. She promoted the military escalation in Iraq, engineered the military build-up (pivot to Asia) against China and negotiated the continued presence of thousands of US troops in Afghanistan.

Clinton has repeatedly pledged to her supporter Haim Saban and Israeli Prime Minister Benyamin Netanyahu that she will give Israel "all the necessary military, diplomatic, economic and moral support it needs to vanquish Hamas" regardless of the many thousands of Palestinian civilian casualties. The 'pragmatic feminist' Hillary is a fervent supporter of Saudi despotism and its genocidal war against the popular forces in Yemen. Hillary tried to pressure President Obama to send US ground troops into Syria. She promotes the continuation of harsh trade sanctions against Russia.

Trump opposes any further direct US intervention in the Middle East. During his debate in South Carolina, he repeatedly denounced President George W. Bush's invasion of Iraq as based on 'deliberate lies to the American people', to the shock and horror of the Republican Party elite. He opposes sending ground troops overseas to Europe or Asia, which imposes a huge financial burden on the US taxpayers. He has gone on to suggest that European and Asian powers can and should pay for their own defense. Trump argues that the US could work with Putin against radical Islamist terrorism and he regards Russia as a potential trading partner. His anti-interventionism has been labeled as 'isolationist by the Plutocratic Zionist ideologues and militarist warlords holed up in their Washington think tanks, but Trump's 'America First' resonates profoundly with the war-weary and economically devastated US electorate.

Israel

Clinton has totally and unconditionally pledged to widen and deepen US subordination to Israel's war aims in the Middle East and to defend Israel's war crimes against the Palestinian people in the occupied territories and within apartheid Israel. As a result, Clinton has built a coalition made-up of unsavory mafia-linked, gambling, media and speculator billionaires, whose first loyalty is not to America but Israel. She denounces all critics of Israel as 'anti-Semites'.

Trump has never been a critic of Israel but he has called for greater 'even-handedness', which is anathema within Zionist circles. For that reason he has secured only a single Plutocratic Zionismt supporter, Sheldon Adelson— whose calls for more Zionist support for Trump appear to have fallen on deaf ears. So far, he has not been labelled an anti-Semite ... perhaps because his own daughter converted to Judaism following her marriage. But his lack of effusive philo-Zionism has him marked as 'unreliable' to the Jewish State. As a subterfuge for his lack of servility to Tel Aviv, some Democratic Party Zionist hacks emphasize his 'racism' and 'fascist' tendencies.

The Democratic Elections: The Real Muck

Clinton currently leads Sanders for the Democratic nomination mostly on the basis of non-elected delegates, the so-called 'super delegates', who are party loyalists appointed by the bosses and elite politicians. Sanders' call for a "political revolution in America" will have no traction unless there is first a political revolution within the Democratic Party. But the Democratic Party is like the Augean Stable—a cleanup requiring a Herculean effort and a loud pugnacious leader with a big broom. Senator Sanders is no Hercules.

As a positive beginning, Sanders has mobilized grass roots support, raised progressive health, education, and tax policies that adversely affect Clinton's billionaire Wall Street backers (big financier Jaime Diamond called Sanders 'the most dangerous man in America'), and secured millions of contributions from small donors. But he has failed to target and demand the exit of the Plutocratic Zionists, the Wall Street bankers, and speculators and venal black politicians controlling the Democratic Party. They run the elections of US presidents and will make sure Hillary Clinton secures the nomination by hook or (more likely) crook.

Clinton is backed by this formidable authoritarian

(profoundly anti-democratic) electoral machine. She is totally embedded in the process. Clinton has a track record of enthusiastic support for the barbarism of torture, laughing at and cheering on the torture-death of the wounded Libyan leader, Muammar Gadhafi. In the pursuit of wars and war crimes, Hillary Clinton knows no limit and has borne no accountability. What makes Hillary so terrifyingly dangerous is that she could be Commander in Chief of a great military power. While Clinton may be no Hitler, the US is vastly more engaged in world politics than Weimer Germany ever was. Her dictate would bring on global destruction.

If the Democratic primaries are as profoundly undemocratic as they have been in the past, the Republicans and their plutocrat partners are openly planning and plotting to 'Dump the Donald' and prevent Trump from obtaining an electoral victory. They have been discussing ways to use convention procedures to undermine a majority vote, and set up a 'brokered convention', where the 'big-wigs' jigger the delegates, rules and voting procedures behind closed doors robbing the populist front-runner of his party candidacy.

Conclusion

The US presidential primaries reveal in all their facets the decay and corruption of democracy in an era of imperial decline. The financial oligarchy in the Democratic Party, backing a psychopathic militarist, like Hillary, cannot disguise her track record by labeling their candidate a pragmatist; the majority of Sanders supporters have no illusions about Clinton. Panic and hysteria among an unsavory elite in the Republican Party and its efforts to block a *sui-generis* conservative Republican isolationist speaks to the fragility of imperial rule.

The psychopathic warmonger Clinton cannot be considered the pragmatic lesser evil to Donald Trump or any

Republican their bosses decide to spew out. At best, she might be the equal evil. In this case, fewer than 50% of the electorate may vote. If, after being robbed of his growing movement for the Democratic Party candidacy, Bernie Sanders, does not break out with an independent bid for the White House, I will join the miniscule 1% who vote for Green Party candidate, Dr. Jill Stein.

PART TWO

THE DELUSION
OF EMPIRE

| Chapter Six |

ANGLO-AMERICA: REGRESSION AND REVERSION IN THE MODERN WORLD

Introduction

What does it mean when the US and British financial systems launder hundreds of billions of dollars of illicit funds stolen by world leaders while their governments turn a 'blind eye', and yet the very same Anglo-American officials investigate, prosecute, fine and arrest officials from rival governments, rival banks and political leaders for corruption?

What does it mean when the US government expands a world-wide network of nuclear missiles on bases stretching from Poland, Bulgaria, Romania, the Gulf States to Japan, surrounding Russia, Iran and China, while the very same US and NATO officials investigate and condemn rival defense officials from Russia, China and Iran, as military threats to peace and stability?

What does it mean when Anglo-American economic officials devote decades to raising the age of retirement, reducing working and middle class household income, cutting workers compensation, expanding part-time work, setting the stage for mass layoffs slashing unemployment and health benefits and reducing social spending by the hundreds of billions of dollars and then turn around and investigate and threaten rival countries, like China and Argentina with loss of markets, investment and employment for not doing the same thing ?

The meaning of Anglo-America's long-term, large-scale structural regression is clearly evident across the world. From Europe to Latin America and from Asia to Africa, socio-economic and politico-military agendas have been reversed.

Since the end of the Second World War there had been incremental gains in labor rights, stable employment, poverty reduction and working conditions.

Recently, these have all been reversed: Longer working days and weeks with reduced salaries and benefits; unstable temporary work replaces stable employment; employer-funded pensions are eliminated and replaced by multi-billion dollar corporate tax cuts and off-shore tax evasion.

Systematic structural swindles by the leading financial institutions have forced employees to delay retirement for years in order to 'self-finance' their own meager 'pensions', some expecting to 'die at the job'.

Capitalist regression has been implemented by arbitrary state dictates and authoritarian decrees, erasing any pretense of democratic procedures and constitutional laws.

The regressive and retrograde leader-states from the imperial centers impose their conditions on follower regimes like Mexico and Russia forcing them to reverse their legacy of social progress while blackmailing these regimes' oligarchs with the loss of lucrative markets, access to tax and money-laundering havens, and impunity for their crimes and swindles.

Anglo-America: Historic Reversion

For the past three decades, the US and Great Britain have led the global drive to undermine labor's advances. First, the economic structure sustaining labor organizations were dismantled and fragmented. Then organized labor was decimated, co-opted and corporatized.

Capital proceeded to reverse labor and social welfare legislation and lower wages, in order to impose longer workdays and destabilize employment.

The mass media re-packaged the regression cycle as *'economic reform'*, a euphemism, which disguised the re-concentration of power, wealth and income over the last three decades.

The growth of inequality and the concentration of wealth and assets to the 1% became 'the standard' for the Anglo-American era. However, class organization and the vicissitudes of class struggles continued to constrain efforts to impose unchallenged Anglo-American capitalist rulership throughout the world.

The first decisive blow against social reform resulted from the systematic Anglo-American breakdown of the former USSR and allied nations of the Warsaw Pact in East Europe. This was followed by the endogenous dissolution of Communist Party rule in China, Russia, Eastern Europe, the Baltic and Balkan states and their conversion into capitalist satellites. Social welfare, full employment, public pensions and health systems were shredded; labor lost all its rights except one—the right to emigrate to the West as cheap labor.

From Russia to Latvia and Poland to Bulgaria and Romania, there were massive layoffs, plant closures and the total dissolution of social security networks driven by the Anglo-America neo-liberal onslaught. The Atlantic Alliance brought their new Eastern satellites to social submission.

Until the second decade of the 21st century, Western Europe's centers for the defense of the progressive social agenda were in France, Italy, Spain, Greece and Portugal. The social agenda in Latin America and China faced the Anglo-America offensive even earlier.

France: The Strategic Key to Anglo-American Social Regression

France has been the center where the Anglo-American regressive attack on socio-economic policy and Southern Europe's resistance has been playing out.

By 2015 the regressive alliance had overturned all progressive social policy in the former communist bloc countries. Their alliance with Germany's finance sector give them tight control of the EU and they successfully decimated the progressive social programs and labor legislation in Greece, Spain and Portugal.

France became the centerpiece for Western capitalism's drive to incorporate Italy into the regressive orbit. The conquest of France and Italy would completely reverse 70 years of incremental labor gains after the defeat of fascist capitalism.

The assault on France's progressive social agenda is spearheaded by the *retro-Socialist* President Francois Holland and his troika of authoritarian hyper-capitalist ministers: Financial Minister Michel Sapin, Prime Minister Manuel Valls and Economy Minister Emmanuel Macron.

The strategy of relying on a *'nominal socialist'* to destroy the social welfare state is a classic *'Trojan Horse'* operation. Hollande's virulent anti-labor policy is implemented *by decree* under a joint plan developed in association with France's leading industrialists.

The imposition of the regressive policy in France

began in stages. It first established the retrograde political leadership with Valls, a notorious authoritarian police-state official willing to over-ride any democratic niceties. The Economy Minister, Emanuel Macron, a millionaire investment banker, is a direct associate of the financial elite, with no qualms in slashing labor programs. The Finance Minister Michel Sapin, a long-time accomplice of the French bureaucratic-capitalist elite, is prepared to slash pensions and public services while reducing job security in order to lower the cost of labor to capital.

Once Hollande and his Troika took control of the centers of political power, (and after militarizing French society in response to the terrorist attacks), the regime launched its anti-labor offensive to shred the progressive social agenda. Its first target was its most formidable – the mass of the French working class.

Declaring 'anti-ISIS' martial law powers, Hollande adopted an outright authoritarian strategy, bypassing the elected French Parliament in the legislature and imposed *'rule by decree'* with the announcement of a highly regressive labor law against the French people.

The dictatorial labor decree was a first step to weaken organized labor's capacity to protect wages and job security in order to give a powerful impetus to employer control over the French labor force.

Once Hollande's labor decree established capitalist supremacy, his Troika would be in a decisive position to reverse seventy years of incremental social advances.

The joint Hollande-Troika-capitalist bloc emasculated the legislature, leaving a weak, bleating chorus of so-called *'left Socialists'* to bemoan their political impotence. Then an entirely new business anti-labor code was rolled out, which included the right of bosses to hire and fire workers at will, extend the workday, lengthen the work week, undermine labor's bargaining power and restrain strikes and job actions. This would open the way for a wave of irregular and contingent jobs for new workers. Using the pretext of terrorist attacks, the French capitalist class had begun to rule by decree to further expand and deepen their long planned assault on labor.

Hollande's Troika and France's capitalists are lowering corporate taxes and employer contribution to social payments. Regulations that restrained the concentration of elite power were eliminated.

With curfews and *'anti-terrorist'* militarized police in the streets, French business elite could now freely begin to to imitate the Anglo-American capitalist elite and impose an iron-fisted New Order.

Without labor constraints on French capital, the bosses are is free to relocate factories and investments any and everywhere, under the most favorable wage, tax, employment and environmental conditions.

No longer required to invest in French industry, the business elite can transfer capital from industry to financial sectors, allowing hundreds of billions of euros to be laundered in off shore tax havens.

The Hollande troika will now also establish its own version of 'Security and Exchange investigators' to prosecute and fine its rival Anglo-American financial swindlers, just as the Anglo-Americans pursue their French competitors today.

The Hollande regime's regressive social agenda has opened the door for an even more extreme Presidential prototype to follow and Alain Juppe is waiting.

The rabid Republican Party presidential candidate, Alain Juppe, promises to go 'whole hog' in utterly destroying the French welfare state, as it has existed since the fall of fascism. If elected president, Juppe promised to slash 100 billion euros from the budget—double the amount that the

Hollande regime currently seeks to cut. Juppe has pledged to eliminate 250,000 civil service jobs in all vital social sectors; to delay the retirement age from 62 to 65; eliminate the 35-hour workweek; facilitate worker layoffs and decimate unemployment benefits. Finally, Juppe has promised French capital that he would implement their entire business agenda, cut taxes for business and bankers and eliminate the tax on inheritance implemented nearly four decades ago.

In other words, the Hollande regime's assault on labor and embrace of business has opened the door for the rise of the extreme right. Moreover, Hollande has manipulated the incidents of Islamist terrorism to assume arbitrary decree powers wiping out any pretense of a democratic government. The terrorist incidents are arguably related to Hollande's colonialist embrace of the 'regime change' assaults against the secular nationalist governments of Libya and Syria and his policy of sending (or tolerating the recruitment of) marginalized French youth of North African ancestry to fight in the ensuing civil wars. This has further strengthened the rise of the extreme right in France.

As the Socialist and Republicans compete for dictatorial powers to serve business' regressive agenda, the nationalist, protectionist and social reformist policies of the National Front are emerging as the populist alternative in the coming presidential race. Anti-fascist rhetoric has worn thin and important sectors of the working class will turn to the National Front in defense of their jobs and social legislation. The anti-immigration rhetoric of the National Front is now part of the political vocabulary of the Republicans as well as Prime Minister Valls.

The only alternative to a power grab by the French hard right is a mass general strike and sustained street battles in order to resist the reaction by decree.

As throughout history, popular struggles in France

begin in the streets—among the trade unions and young workers angrily facing low wages, austerity and the grim prospect of 'permanently' temporary jobs.

The outcome of the intensifying French labor-capital conflict will have a decisive impact on the future of labor throughout Europe, especially among all Left unionists.

Latin America: The Labor-Capital Showdown

Beyond Europe, the Anglo-American onslaught against labor and the working class resonates most directly in Latin America and to a lesser extent in Asia and Africa.

The first country to fall victim to capital's attack was Mexico with the implementation of the North America Free Trade Agreement (NAFTA). By the early 1990's NAFTA had demolished the independent Mexican trade unions, crippled social legislation, eliminated subsidies to small corn farmers, forced peasants into debt, reduced minimum wage, doubled poverty levels and turned the majority of the labor force into landless, indebted, casual workers. On the other hand, NAFTA has been a bottomless source of wealth as capitalists accumulate double and triple digit profits and absolute power to hire and fire employees. Mexico's government, under Anglo-American capital, has allowed the illicit transfer of hundreds of billions of dollars of Mexican assets to US, English and other overseas banks, which have become immense money-laundering operations. The proximity of Mexican drug cartels to the US banks has facilitated the extension of their networks into the US market. The horrific expansion of drug cartel death squads, linked to Mexico's political leaders, dates from the 1990s and the signing of NAFTA. This bloody nexus has consolidated neoliberal political power in Mexico and weakened the possibility of a viable mass electoral alternative.

Anglo-American dominance in Latin America in the 1990's led to an entire panoply of regressive policies: privatizing and denationalizing the most lucrative natural and state resources, banks and industries; reducing wages and social spending for labor while increasing the concentration of capital. By 2001, however, the Anglo-American edifice collapsed throughout South America with the demise of its neo-liberal political leadership.

From Venezuela in 1999, to Argentina in 2003, Brazil 2003, Bolivia 2006 and Ecuador 2007, left and center-left parties capitalized on their mass support and were elected into power. They took advantage of global economic conditions with the rising commodity prices, booming Chinese markets and new regional alliances to fund a variety of progressive social agendas, including increased social expenditures, guaranteed pensions, family allowances, minimum wages, wage increases for public sector and expanded labor rights.

The Anglo-American power elite was in retreat and isolated, but it was far from defeated. They retrenched and prepared to re-mobilize their strategic business, banking and political allies when the opportunity arose. They counter-attacked when global and regional conditions turned unfavorable to the social regimes.

The assault on Latin America was preceded by the Anglo-American neo-liberal take-over of Northern Europe from the 1990s to the first decade of the 21st century. This was followed by the sweep and grab of the Balkans and Southern Europe. The combined Anglo-American-EU-NATO offensive now seeks to reverse the last social-welfare regimes in Europe: France and Italy with the help of President Hollande and Prime Minister Renzi.

Simultaneously the Anglo-American offensive has been launched throughout Latin America. Their goal is to recover the imperial prerogatives, political power and economic privileges lost during the previous decade. The primary Euro-American target is the *'golden triangle'*, Argentina, Brazil and Venezuela. These countries constitute a global center of immense oil and agro-mineral wealth.

The Argentine neo-liberal restoration took off in December 2015 with the election of far-right President Mauricio Macri. His junta wasted no time in stripping the state of its social legislation, dismantling job security through large-scale layoffs and assuming authoritarian rule by decree to devalue Argentina's currency by 40% and to eliminate state subsidies and raising the price for gas, electricity, transport, and water between 300 and 800%.

The regressive offensive was in full force. Next, Brazil's twice elected President Dilma Rousseff was 'impeached' and essentially overthrown by a bizarre legislative right-wing coup-d'état, designed to reverse a generation of progressive regulatory, labor and employment legislation. It was also secretly designed to halt corruption investigations against many right-wing politicians.

Venezuela is next. It will be the scene of a full-scale-elite coup-d'état with imperial backing, to overthrow the government of President Maduro and end decades of progressive social advances under the Chavista governments.

While in France and Italy the great social reversal is being implemented by internal enemies from the 'progressive' political parties (Trojan Horses), in Latin America the reversal is led by openly hostile class enemies who depend on the arbitrary exercise of executive power. The drive to put a definitive end to the *'welfare state'* in Europe and Latin America is marked by the use of dictatorial decrees, (in the style of Mussolini in the 1920s) as exercised by Argentina's elected President Marci in January 2016 and Brazil's 'Interim (Coup) President' Temer in April 2016. Meanwhile capitalist lockouts, hoarding and sabotage are being used to crush Venezuela's elected government.

This epochal confrontation has spread across Africa and Asia. China's capitalist offensive has seen a four-fold increase in the number of new billionaires in less than a decade, at the expense of hundreds of millions of workers stripped of their rights and social programs.

South Africa, under the ANC government, turned its back on social gains promised by the liberation struggle and has imposed regressive social legislation and repressive anti-labor decrees. A corrupt class of black and white billionaires now rule by guns and clubs over the black working class.

In Africa and the Middle East, the social welfare states of the nationalist regimes in Iraq and Libya have been completely shredded through imperialist military intervention and civil war. Their once advanced societies have been thrown back into ethno-tribal warfare with no remaining modern social institutions in those two blighted, resource-rich nations.

Wither the Class Struggle: Historical Reversal and Class Revolt?

The Anglo-American offensive to reverse decades of social advance has captured most of Europe. They have incorporated or coopted the Social Democratic parties and are moving swiftly toward dismantling the decade-long center-left welfare states in Latin America.

In Africa, the centerpiece of Anglo-Americanization is South Africa, the continent's most advanced bastion of international capitalism.

In Asia, China, the second most important capitalist economy in the world, has been leading the struggle to overturn the social agenda of the revolutionary past.

Large-scale, prolonged class resistance in several decisive centers is emerging to confront this Anglo-American process of reversion. The class confrontation however takes specific characteristics in each country.

In France, the major protagonists of street fighting and marches are young unemployed or casual workers, members of the strategic transport and oil unions and student-workers facing a bleak future of marginal employment and a shredded social safety net.

Trade unions and farmers' association have joined the street struggles on numerous occasions, possibly in preparation for a general strike.

In Latin America, the center of the class struggle is Argentina. Power-mad President Macri immediately imposed regressive policies against all sectors of the working class. His actions managed to unite the four major trade union confederations, multiple retirees associations and small businesspeople bankrupted by exorbitant charges on gas and electrical use and regional neighborhood federations. The widespread growth of job actions among public sector employees points to a general strike.

The regressive assault on long-term social legislation in Brazil immediately followed the thinly disguised capitalist coup. The ousting of President Rousseff has provoked street demonstrations, led by the huge rural landless workers movement (MST), the confederation of industrial and service workers (CUT), social movements of the homeless workers and the recipients of Lula's poverty programs. New revelations, based on taped conversations among the coup plotters reveal their plans to oust the incumbent President Rousseff in order to derail official investigations into their own corruption scandals. This has enraged the general public.

With the initial take-over, the Brazilian political-financial elite has prepared to launch its full-scale reversal of pensions and employment laws and wage guarantees. The pro-business leadership plans to slash corporate and wealth taxes and to appoint business executives to all leading ministries. The deep corruption scandal and the mass demonstrations suggest the rightwing power grab may not survive.

The regressive offensive in Venezuela has severely crippled the national economy and deeply eroded living standards of the vast majority of the working class. The rightist Congress, backed by the US and allied with international mass media, industry and multinational banks, are trying to force the resignation of Socialist President Maduro.

Maduro has declared a state of emergency and mobilized the armed forces. He called on the military and popular militia to defend the constitutional order and has threatened to mobilize the workers to "take control of the means of production". Still, the leftist government vacillates over arming the militias and workers. A wide gap remains before the word and the deed.

In the meantime Venezuela's right wing and left-wing mass mobilizations face each other in the streets seething with class hatred and waiting to engage in a decisive confrontation. The military thus far remains constitutionalist and on the side of the elected president.

In South Africa, the corrupt pro-business ANC led by President Zuma murdered dozens of striking mine workers. It has impoverished millions of shantytown residents, while increasing the wealth and power of the black-white elite. On April 30, 2016, 1.1.million South African activists, including civil society and community organizations and trade unions covering the mining, manufacturing and service sectors have organized to form a new confederation linked with informal, unemployed and poor workers. The South African Workers Summit replaces the moribund and corrupt labor confederation, COSATU, the 'labor desk' for the neo-liberal ANC regime. The new confederation will co-ordinate mass struggles and reclaim social programs as a central part of the anti-capitalist revolution.

In China, the growth and consolidation of the world's second largest concentration of billionaires has led to the proliferation of large-scale industrial workers' strikes, walkouts and confrontations with factory bosses, company unions and government officials. China is becoming the epicenter of Asia's working class struggles. Chinese workers have forced the government to investigate and jail over 200,000 corrupt officials, high and low, and to concede substantial wage increases and social compensation to factory workers. Fearing more social upheaval, China's billionaires and multi-millionaires have transferred hundreds of billions of dollars of stolen assets abroad in a buying spree of high-end property in the 'safe' Anglo-American "heartland" of world reaction.

The continued advance of working class struggles against the public and private oligarchs has forced the Chinese Prime Minister to reform elite privileges and prosecute large-scale banking swindles and illegal seizure of farmland. Especially important, millions of workers have successfully secured double-digit wage increases and the right to legally live in urban/industrial and construction centers.

As it gains momentum, class struggle in China can become the centerpiece for a wider Asian social transformation and a great leap forward to socialist values.

Conclusion

The Anglo-American drive to establish a global regressive social order has pushed billions of workers on five continents into destitution, insecurity and lifelong exploitation. The capitalist world rules by fiat and violence, declaring that social regression and worker repression are the 'wave of the future'. For the elite, the proper order of the universe is being 'restored'!

In response, new working class organizations have emerged and engage directly to defend their historic social advances and economic rights.

In the course of defending their past progressive social legacy, the new working class militants can clearly see the imperative to challenge and overthrow the entire political and economic order. From France to Latin America, from China to South Africa, class struggle is defining the present and future of class relations.

| Chapter Seven |

THE MOTE REMAINS IN THE EMPEROR'S EYE

Post-colonial empires are complex organizations. They are organized on a multi-tiered basis, ranging from relatively autonomous national and regional allies to subservient vassal states, with variations in between.

In the contemporary period, the idea of empire does not operate as a stable global structure, though it may aspire and strive for such. While the US is the major imperial power, it does not dominate some leading global political-economic and military powers, such as Russia and China.

Imperial powers, like the US, have well-established regional satellites but have also suffered setbacks and retreats from independent local economic and political challengers.

Empire is not a fixed structure rigidly embedded in military or economic institutions. It contains sets of competing forces and relations, which can change over time and circumstances. Moreover, imperial allies and clients do not operate through fixed patterns of submission. While there is submission to general agreements on ideology, military doctrine and economic policy identified by and in the interest of imperial rulers, there are cases of vassal states pursuing their own links with non-imperial markets, investors and exporters.

If the global world of imperial power is complex and indeterminate to some degree, so is the internal political, economic, administrative and military structure of the imperial state. The imperial political apparatus has become more heavily weighted on the side of security institutions than diplomatic and representative bodies. Economic institutions are organized for overseas markets dominated by multinational corporations against local markets and producers. The 'market economy' is a misnomer.

Military-security institutions and budgets utilize most state functionaries and public resources, subordinating markets and diplomatic institutions to military priorities.

While imperial state operations function through their military and civilian administrative apparatus, there are competitive socio-political class, ethnic, and military configurations to consider.

In analyzing the effective or real power of the principle institutions of the imperial state, one must distinguish between goals and results, purpose and actual performance. Often commentators make sweeping statements about 'imperial power and dominance', while in fact, some policies may have ended in costly losses and retreats due to specific national, local or regional alignments.

Hence it is crucial to look closely at the imperial interaction between an empire's various tiers of allies and adversaries in order to understand the immediate and long-term structures and direction of imperial state policy.

This chapter will first describe the leader-follower imperial relationships in four zones: US, Western Europe, and Canada; the Asia-Pacific; Middle East and Africa; and Latin America; and identify the terrain of struggles and conflict. This will be followed by an examination of the contemporary 'map of empire'. We will then contrast the alignment of forces between Western imperial allies and their current adversaries. In the final section we will look at the sources of fragmentation between the imperial state and economic globalization as well as the fissures and fallout between imperial allies and followers.

Tiers of Imperial Allies in the West

Western imperialism is a complex pyramidal structure where the dominant United States interacts through a five-tier system. There is a vertical and horizontal configuration of leader and follower states that cannot be understood through simplistic 'solar system' metaphors of centers, semi-peripheries and peripheries.

Western imperial power extends and overlaps from the first tier to the second, that is, from the United States to France, England, Germany, Italy and Canada. The scope and depth of US military, bureaucratic, political, and economic institutions form the framework within which the followers operate.

The second tier of empire ties the top tier to the bottom tiers by providing military support and economic linkages, while securing autonomous levers to enlarge its own geo-political spheres.

The third tier of imperialism in the West comprises Poland, Scandinavia, the Low Countries and Baltic States. These are geographically and economically within the sphere of Western Europe and militarily dependent on US-NATO military dominance. The third tier is a heterogeneous group, ranging from highly advanced and sophisticated welfare-states like Sweden, Norway, Denmark, Holland, and Belgium to relatively backward Baltic dependencies like Latvia, Estonia, Lithuania, and Poland. They exercise few independent power initiatives and depend on protection from the Tier 1 and 2 imperial centers.

Tier four states include countries like Greece, Spain,

Portugal, Hungary, Czech Republic, Slovakia, Bulgaria, and Romania. These are essentially satellite nations, who follow the leader imperial countries, providing bases, troops and tourist resorts. In general, they have no independent voice or decision-making presence in regional or global conflicts. Despite their instability and the occasional outbursts of radical dissent, the lower tier countries have yet to break with the higher tiers controlled by the EU and NATO hierarchy.

The fifth-tier satellites include recently fabricated mini-states like Albania, Kosovo, Macedonia, Slovenia and Croatia, which act as military bases, tourist havens and economic dependencies. They are the outcome of the first-tier and second-tier policies of regime change and state dismemberment through NATO-led wars designed to destroy any remnant of the multi-ethnic social welfare states, and to degrade Russian influence, especially in Yugoslavia.

Mapping the leader-follower structure of the Western empire depends on the distribution of military resources and their location along the Russian border. The US-EU Empire faces the problem of meeting rising economic demands from the multi-tiered empire, which has exceeded their capacity to fulfill. This had led to shifting trade alliances and independent pressure to 'go beyond' the dictates of the imperial leaders.

Leader imperial states have tightened economic and political control over their followers—especially when the military consequences of empire have disrupted everyday life, security and the economy. An ongoing example is the flood of millions of desperate refugees entering Europe as a result of US imperial war policies in the Middle East and North Africa. This mass influx threatens the political and social stability of Europe. Following the US putsch in the Ukraine and the inevitable response from Moscow,

Washington ordered an economic blockade of Russia. The economic consequences of US-imposed sanctions against the giant Russian market has severely affected European exports, especially agriculture and heavy industry, and caused instability in the energy market, which was dominated by the now banned Russian petroleum and gas producers.

The Eastern Empire

The US imperial design in East Asia is vastly different in structure, allies and adversaries from that in the West. The leaders and followers are very heterogeneous in the East. The multi-tier US Empire in Asia is designed to undermine and eventually dominate North Korea and China.

Since the Second World War, the US has been the center of the Pacific empire. It also suffered serious military setbacks in Korea and Indo-China. With the aid of its multi-tiered auxiliaries, the US has recovered its influence in Indo-China and South Korea.

The US position, as the first-tier imperial power, is sustained by second-tier imperial allies, such as Australia, New Zealand, India, and Japan.

These second-tier allies are diverse entities. For example, the Indian regime is a reticent latecomer to the US Empire and still retains a higher degree of autonomy in dealing with China. In contrast, while Australia and New Zealand retained their dependent military ties with the US, they are increasingly dependent on Chinese commodity markets and investments. Japan, a powerful traditional economic ally of the US, remains a weak military satellite of the US-Asian Empire.

Third-tier countries include South Korea, Taiwan, Philippines, Malaysia, Thailand, and Indonesia. Despite the fact that it is the US's most important military dependency,

South Korea has moved steadily closer to the Chinese market, as has the populous Indonesian Republic.

Taiwan, while a military dependency of the US, has stronger ethnic and economic links to China than to the US.

The Philippines is a backward US military vassal-state and former colony, which retains its legacy as an imperial enclave against China. Thailand and Malaysia have remained as third-tier imperial auxiliaries, subject to occasional nationalist or democratic popular upsurges.

The fourth-tier countries within the US East Asian Empire are the least reliable because they are relatively new associates. Vietnam, Cambodia, Laos and Myanmar have transformed from independent statist economies to US-Japanese and Chinese-centered markets, financial and military dependencies.

The US Empire has focused on confronting China through its military, controlling South China trading routes and trying to form regional economic trade agreements, which exclude China. However, the imperial multi-tiered structure has been mostly limited to various US military harassments and joint 'war games' exercises with US clients and 'allies'. This has had minimal economic input from even their closest allies. The US Eastern Empire has lost significant economic counterparts because of its confrontational approach to China. Its provocative trade pacts have failed to undermine China's dynamic economy and trade.

The US Eastern Empire may dominate its multi-tiered allies, vassals and recent converts through its military. It may succeed in provoking a serious military confrontation with China. But it has failed to re-establish a dominant structure within Asia to sustain US imperial superiority in the event of a war.

China drives the growth and dynamism of Asia and is the vital market for regional products as well as a crucial supplier of minerals, precious metals, industrial products, high tech, and service activity throughout the region.

The US has occasionally turned to its 'fifth-tier' allies among non-state entities in Tibet and Hong Kong, and among ethno-Islamist terrorist-separatist groups in Western China, using human rights propaganda, but these have had no significant impact in weakening China or undermining its regional influence.

The Eastern Empire can wield none of the economic leverage on China that the Western empire is able to deploy against Russia. China has established more effective economic relations in Asia than Russia has with the West. However, Russia has greater military capability and a more committed political will to push back Western imperial military threats than China. In recent years, Beijing has adopted a policy of strengthening its high tech military and maritime capabilities. In the wake of the US putsch in the Ukraine and the West's economic sanctions against Russia, Moscow has been forced to bolster strategic military-economic ties with China. Joint security exercises between Russia and China, as well as greater trade, pose formidable counter-weights to the multi-tiered alliances linking the US and EU to Japan, Australia, and South Korea.

In other words, the diverse geographic multi-tiered US imperial structures in the East do not and cannot dominate a strategic top-tiered alliance of Russia and China, despite their lack of other strong military allies and client states.

If we look beyond European and Asian spheres of its empire to the Middle East and Latin America, the US imperial presence is subject to rapidly evolving power relations. We cannot simply add or subtract from the US and Russian and Chinese rivalries, because these do not necessarily add up to a new 'imperial' or 'autonomous' center of power.

Imperial Power in the Middle East: The Multi-Tiered Empire in Retreat

The US empire in the Middle East occupies a pivotal point between West and East; between the top and secondary tiers of empire; between Islamic and anti-Islamic alliances.

If we extend the 'Middle East' to include South Asia and North Africa we capture the dimensions of the Western imperial quest for supremacy in this region.

The empire in the Middle East reflects US and Western European tiers of power as they interact with local counterparts and satellite states.

The US-EU top tiers link their goals of encircling and undermining Russia and regional adversaries, like Iran, with the regional ambitions of their NATO ally, Turkey.

Imperial powers in the Middle East and North Africa operate through local allies, auxiliaries and satellites as they compete for territorial fragments and power bases following the US 'wars for regime changes'.

With the US at the top, the European Union, Israel, Turkey and Saudi Arabia comprise the second-tier allies. Egypt, Tunisia, Iraq and Jordan, which are financial and political dependencies of the empire, rank as third-tier. The fourth-tier includes the Gulf States, the Kurdish war lords, Lebanese and Yemeni local puppets of the Saudi monarchy, and Israel's client Palestinian Bantustan in the West Bank.

Saudi and Western-funded regional terrorist groups aspire to fourth-tier membership once a successful 'regime change' has been achieved, leading to territorial fragmentation in Syria. The terrorist enclaves are located in Syria, Iraq, and Libya and play a multi-purpose role in undermining adversaries in order to restore imperial dominance.

The Middle East Empire is the least stable region and the most susceptible to internal rivalries.

Israel exercises a unique and unrivaled voice in securing US financial and military resources and political support for its brutal colonial control over Palestine and Syrian territories and captive populations. Saudi Arabia finances and arms autonomous Islamist terrorist groups as part of their policy of advancing the kingdom's political-territorial designs in Pakistan, Yemen, Afghanistan, Iraq, Syria, Iran, and the Gulf. Turkey has its own regional ambitions and terrorist mercenaries. Within this volatile context, the US Empire finds itself competing with its auxiliaries for control over the same Middle East clients.

The Middle East Empire is fraught with powerful adversaries at each point of contention. The huge, independent nation of Iran stands as a powerful obstacle to the West, the Saudis, and Israel, and competes for influence among satellites in the Gulf, Yemen, Iraq, Syria, and Lebanon. Hezbollah, a powerful nationalist group within Lebanon, has played a crucial role defending Syria against dismemberment and is linked with Iran against Israeli intervention. Russia has military and trade relations with Syria and Iran in opposition to the Western imperial alliance. Meanwhile, the US imperial satellite states in Afghanistan, Iraq, Libya, and Egypt are rapidly disintegrating in the face of gross corruption, Islamist resurgence, policy incompetence, and economic crises.

To speak formally of a 'Western empire' in vast sections of the Middle East and North Africa is a misnomer for several reasons:

- In Afghanistan, the Nationalist-Islamist Taliban and its allies control most of the country, except for a few garrison cities.
- Yemen, Libya, and Iraq are battleground states, contested terrain with nothing remotely resembling a functioning imperial domain. Iraq is under siege from

the North by Kurds, the center by ISIS, the South by nationalist Shi'a militias and mass organizations in contention with grossly corrupt US imperial-backed puppets in Baghdad.
- The US-EU mercenaries in Syria have been defeated by Syrian-Russian-Hezbollah-Iranian forces aided by independent Kurds.
- Israel behaves more like a militarist 'settler' predator usurping historical Palestine than a reliable imperial collaborator.

So far, the empire project in the Middle East and North Africa has been the costliest and least successful for Western imperialism. First and foremost, responsibility for the current Middle East imperial debacle falls directly on the top tier political and military leaders who have pursued policies and strategies (regime change and national dismemberment) incompatible with the imperial precepts that normally guide empires.

The top tier of the US imperial-military elite follows Israeli military prerogatives, as dictated by the Zionist Power Configuration (ZPC) embedded within the US state apparatus. Their policy has been to destroy Islamic and Arab-nationalist structures and institutions of power—not conquer and reconfigure them to be absorbed into Western imperial institutions ... as the US was able to do in Asia and Europe. This parrots the Israeli-settler policy of 'erasure' and has made the region totally unstable for imperial trade. The wanton dismemberment of the whole social-political-security institutional structure of Iraq is a prime example of the Israeli policy of 'erasure' promoted by US Zionist advisers on a grand scale. The same advisers remain within the top tier imperial decision-making apparatus despite 15 years of abject failure.

The Western empire's multi-tier structure, from the US and Western Europe at the top to Kosovo at the bottom, has followed imperial imperatives. In contrast Israeli imperatives direct US military power into perpetual war in the Middle East through the influential ZPC.

This divergent path and the inability to change course and rectify imperial policy has brought disastrous defeats, which have repercussions throughout the global empire, especially freeing up, albeit temporarily, competitors and rivals in Asia and Latin America.

Tiers of Empire in Latin America

The US empire expanded in Central America and the Caribbean during most of the 19th century and reigned supreme in the first half of the 20th century. The exceptions included the nationalist revolutions in Haiti in the early 19th century and Paraguay in the mid-19th century. After the US Civil War, the British Empire in Latin America was replaced by the US, which established a dominant position in the region, except during the successful Mexican Revolution.

Several major challenges have emerged to US imperial domination in the middle of the 20th century:

- The centerpiece of anti-imperialism was the Cuban Revolution in 1959, which provided political, ideological and material backing to a continent-wide challenge.
- Earlier a socialist government emerged in Guyana in 1953 but was overthrown.
- In 1965, the Dominican Revolution challenged a brutal US backed-dictator but was defeated by a direct US invasion.
- In 1970-73 a democratic socialist government was elected in Chile and overthrown by a bloody CIA coup.
- In 1971 a 'workers and peasants' coalition backed a nationalist military government in Bolivia only to be ousted by a US-backed military coup.

- In Argentina (Peron), Brazil (Goulart) and Peru (Alvarez), nationalist-populist governments, opposed to US imperialism, were elected between the middle 1960's to the mid 1970's. Each were overthrown by US-military coups. Apart from the Cuban revolution, the US Empire successfully counter-attacked, relying on US and local business elites to back the military juntas in repressing anti-imperialist and nationalist political parties and movements.

The US Empire re-established its hegemony in the 20th century, based on a multi-tiered military and market directorate, headed at the top by the US. Argentina, Brazil and Chile comprised the second tier, a group of military dictatorships engaged in large-scale state terror and death squad assassinations and forcing hundreds of thousands into exile and prison.

The third tier was based on US surrogates, generals and oligarch-families in Colombia, Venezuela, Peru, Bolivia, Paraguay and Uruguay.

The fourth tier of satellite regimes included Central-America, except Nicaragua, and all of the Caribbean, except Cuba and (briefly) Grenada.

The US Empire ruled through predator allies and satellite oligarchs and successfully imposed a uniform imperial structure based on neoliberal policies. US-centered regional trade, investment and military pacts ensured its imperial supremacy. Through these, they sought to blockade and overthrow the Cuban revolution. The US imperialist system reached its high point between the mid-1970s to the late 1990s—the Golden Age of Plunder. After the pillage of the 1990s, the empire faced a massive wave of challenges from popular uprisings, electoral changes and the collapse of the corrupt auxiliary neoliberal regimes.

The US empire faced powerful challenges from

popular-nationalist regimes from 1999 to 2006 in Venezuela, Argentina, Brazil, Bolivia and Ecuador. Dissident liberal-nationalist governments in Uruguay, Honduras and Paraguay posed their own challenges to imperial control.

The US empire was bogged down in multiple imperial wars in the Middle East (Iraq, Libya, Syria) Asia (Afghanistan) and Europe (Ukraine, Georgia, Yugoslavia), which undermined its capacity to intervene militarily in Latin America.

Cuba, the hemispheric center of anti-imperialist politics, received economic aid from Venezuela and strengthened its diplomatic, trade and security alliances with the anti-interventionist center-left. This provided an impetus to the formation of independent regional trade organizations, which traded heavily with US imperial rivals, China, Iran and Russia, during the commodity boom.

While the US empire in Latin America was in retreat, it had not suffered a strategic defeat because it maintained its powerful business, political and state auxiliary structures, which were ready to regroup and counter-attack at the right moment—the end of the global commodity boom.

By the end of the first decade of the 21st century, the US Empire had counter-attacked, with their political-military clients taking power in the weakest links, Honduras and Paraguay. Since then, neoliberal extremists have been elected to the presidency in Argentina; a corrupt oligarch-led congress has impeached the President of Brazil; and the ground is being prepared to seize control in Venezuela.

The US Empire has re-emerged in Latin America after a decade-long hiatus with a new or re-invigorated multi-tier structure.

At the top tier is the United States, dependent on enforcement of its control through satellite military and business elites among the second-tier countries, Colombia,

Argentina, Brazil, and Mexico. At the third tier are Chile, Peru, Uruguay and the business-political elites in Venezuela, linked to the US and tier-two countries. The fourth tier is dominated by weak submissive regimes in Central America (Panama, Guatemala, Honduras and El Salvador), the Caribbean (especially Santa Domingo, Haiti and Jamaica), and Paraguay.

The US has re-assembled its imperial structure in Latin American rapidly, but creating an assemblage which is extremely fragile, incoherent and subject to disintegration.

The new neoliberal regime in Argentine, the centerpiece of the empire, immediately faces the triple threat of mass unrest, economic crisis, and a weak regime under siege.

Brazil's new US neoliberal constellation of characters are all under indictment for corruption and facing trials, while economic recession and social polarization is undermining their ability to consolidate imperial control.

Venezuela's right wing auxiliaries lack the economic resources to escape the demise of the oil economy, hyperinflation, and the virulent internecine conflicts within the Right.

The US empire in Latin America could best operate through links with the Asian-Pacific trade pact. However, even with new Asian ties, the Latin satellites exhibit none of their Asian counterparts' stability. Moreover, China's dominant economic role in both regions has limited US hegemony over the principal props of the empire.

The Myth of a US Global Empire

The narrative of a US global empire is based on several profound misconceptions, which have distorted the capacity of the US to dominate world politics. The

US regional empires operate in contested universes where powerful counter forces limit imperial dominance.

In Europe, Russia is a powerful counterforce, bolstered by its growing alliances in Asia (China), the Middle East (Iran) and, to a limited extent, by the BRIC countries.

Moreover, Washington's multi-tiered allies in Europe have occasionally followed autonomous policies, which include Germany's oil-gas independent agreements with Russia, eroding US efforts to undermine Moscow.

While it may appear that the imperial military, banking, multi-national corporate structure, at a high level of abstraction, operates within a common imperial enterprise, on issues of everyday policy-making, budgeting, war policies, trade agreements, diplomacy, subversion, and the capitalist marketplace there are multiple countervailing forces.

The empire's multi-tiered allies have their own demands as well as sacrifices they impose on the US imperial center.

Internal members of the imperial structure define competing priorities via domestic power wielders.

The US Empire has extended its military operations to over 700 bases across the world but each operation has been subject to restraints and reversals.

US multinationals have multi-billion dollar operations but they are forced to adjust to the demands of counter-imperial powers (China). They evade almost a trillion dollars of US taxes while absorbing massive assets from the US Treasury in the form of subsidies, infrastructure, and security arrangements.

In sum, while the sun may never set on the purported empire, in pursuit of its actualization, the would-be emperors have little foresight.

| Chapter Eight |

PRESIDENT OBAMA: THE RACE FOR THE IMPERIAL LEGACY

Introduction

President Obama is racing forward to establish his imperial legacy throughout Russia, Asia and Latin America.

In the last two years he has accelerated the buildup of his military nuclear arsenal on the frontiers of Russia. The Pentagon has designed a high tech anti-missile system to undermine Russian defenses.

In Latin America, Obama has shed his shallow pretense of tolerating the center-left electoral regimes. Instead he is has joined with rabid authoritarian neoliberals in Argentina; met with the judges and politicians engineering the overthrow of the democratic Brazilian government; and encouraged the emerging far-right wing regimes in Peru under hardline neoliberal, Pedro Pablo Kuczynski, and in Colombia under President Santos.

In Asia, Obama has clearly escalated a military buildup threatening China's principal waterways in the South China Sea. Obama encouraged aggressive and violent separatist groupings in Hong Kong, Tibet, Xinjian, and Taiwan. Obama invites Beijing billionaires to relocate a trillion dollars in assets to the laundry machines of North America, Europe and Asia. Meanwhile he has actively blocked China's long-planned commercial silk route across Myanmar and west Asia.

In the Middle East, President Obama joined with Saudi Arabia as Riyadh escalated its brutal war and blockade in Yemen. He directed Kenya and other African predator states to attack Somalia. He has continued to back mercenary armies invading Syria while collaborating with the Turkish dictator, Erdogan, as Turkish troops bomb Kurdish fighters who are engaged on the front lines against Islamist terrorism.

President Obama and his minions have consistently groveled before the Jewish State and its US Fifth Column, massively increasing US 'tribute' to Tel Aviv. Meanwhile, Israel continues to seize thousands of acres of Palestinian land, murdering and arresting thousands of Palestinians, from young children to aged grandparents.

The Obama regime is desperate to overcome the consequences of its political, military, and economic failures of the past six years, and establish the US as the uncontested global economic and military power.

At this stage, Obama's supreme goal is to leave an enduring legacy where he will have: (1) surrounded and weakened Russia and China; (2) re-converted Latin America into an authoritarian free-trade backyard for US plunder; (3) turned the Middle East and North Africa into a bloody playpen for Arab and Jewish dictators bent on brutalizing whole nations and turning millions into refugees to flood Europe and elsewhere.

Once this 'legacy' is established, our 'Historic Black President' can boast that he has dragged our 'great nation' into more wars for longer periods of time, costing more diverse human lives, and creating more desperate refugees than any previous US president, all the while polarizing and impoverishing the great mass of working Americans. He will, indeed, set a 'high bar' for his incumbent replacement, Hillary Clinton, to leap over and even expand.

To examine the promise of an Obama legacy and avoid premature judgements, it is best to briefly recall the failures of his first six years and reflect on his current inspired quest for a place in history.

Fear, Loathing and Retreat

Obama's shameless bailout of Wall Street contrasted sharply with the desires and sentiments of the vast majority of Americans who had elected him. This was a historic moment of great fear and loathing where scores of millions of Americans demanded the federal government rein in the financial criminals, stop the downward spiral of household bankruptcies, and home foreclosures, and recover America's working economy. After a brief honeymoon following his 'historic election', the 'historic' President Obama turned his back on the wishes of the people and transferred trillions of public money to bail out the banks and financial centers on Wall Street.

Not satisfied with betraying the American workers and the beleaguered middle class, Obama reneged on his campaign promises to end the war(s) in the Middle East, instead increasing the US troop presence and expanding his drone-assassination warfare against Afghanistan, Iraq, Yemen, Libya, Somalia and Syria.

US troops re-invaded Afghanistan, fought and retreated in defeat. The Taliban advanced. The US expanded its training of the puppet Iraqi army, which collapsed on its first encounters with the Islamic State. Washington retreated again. Regime change in Libya, Egypt and Somalia created predator-mercenary states without any semblance of US control and dominance.

Obama had become a master of both military defeats and financial swindles.

In the Western Hemisphere, a continent of independent Latin American governments had emerged to challenge US supremacy. The 'Historic President' Obama was dismissed as a clueless hack of the US Empire who lacked any rapport with governments south of the Panama Canal. While trade and investment flourished between Latin America and Asia, Washington fell behind. Regional political and economic agreements expanded, leaving Obama without allies.

The Obama administration's clumsy attempts at US-backed regime change were defeated in Venezuela and elsewhere. Only the small, corrupt narco-state of Honduras fell into Obama's orbit with the Hillary Clinton-engineered overthrow of its elected populist-nationalist president.

China and Russia expanded and flourished as commodities boomed, wealth expanded, and demand for Chinese manufactures exploded.

By 2013 Obama had no legacy.

The Recovery: Obama's Lost Legacy

Obama started out on the road to establishing his legacy with the US-financed coup in Ukraine, spearheaded by the first bona fide Nazi militia since WWII. Since celebrating the violent regime change against Ukraine's elected government, Obama's new oligarch-puppet regime and its ethno-nationalist army have been a disaster, losing control of the industrialized Donbass region to ethnic Russian rebels, and completely losing the strategic Crimea when the population overwhelmingly voted to re-join Russia after 50 years. Meanwhile, the oligarch-'president' Poroshenko and his fellow puppets have pilfered several billion dollars in 'aid' from the EU ... all in pursuit of the Obama legacy.

Obama then slapped devastating economic sanctions against Russia for its role in the Crimean referendum and its support for the millions of Russian speakers in Donbass, and in the process forced the European Union to make major trade sacrifices. For their role in creating a real "American legacy" for Mr. Obama, the Germans, French and the other twenty-eight countries have sacrificed billions of Euros in trade and investments, alienating large sectors of their own agricultural and manufacturing economy.

The Obama regime placed nuclear weapons on the Polish border with Russia, pointed at the Russian heartland. Estonians, Lithuanians and Latvians joined Obama's military exercises stationing US ships and attack aircraft in the Baltic Sea, threatening Russia's security.

Obama's Legacy in Latin America

The Obama regime intensified its efforts to re-establish US supremacy with the demise of the center-left regimes following elections in late 2013 to the present.

Obama's 'legacy' in Latin America is based on the return to power of neoliberal elites in the region. Their successful elections were the result of several factors, including: (1) the rise of right wing economic power in Latin America; (2) the decay and corruption of political power within the Left; 3) the incapacity of the Left to develop its own independent mass media to challenge the media monopoly of the right; and (4) the failure of center-left regimes to diversify their economy and develop growth outside the boundaries defined by the dominant capitalist sectors.

The Obama regime worked closely with the

political-business elite, organizing the political campaigns and controlling key economic policies even during the center-Left governments. The left regimes had financed, subsidized and rewarded right-wing business interests in agro-mineral industries, banking, and the media as well as in manufacturing and imports.

As long as worldwide demand for primary materials was strong, the center-left governments had plenty of room to adjust their social spending for workers while accommodating business interests. When demand and prices fell, budget deficits forced the center-left to cut back on social spending for the masses as well as subsidies for the business elite. In response, the business sector organized a full-scale attack on the government in defense of elite power. The Center-Left failed to counter the growing power and position of their business elite adversaries.

The business elite launched a full-scale propaganda war via its captive mass media, focusing on real or imagined corruption scandals discrediting center-left politicians. The Left lacked its own effective mass media to answer the Right's accusations, having failed to democratize the corporate media monopolies.

The center-left parties adopted the elite's technique of financing political campaigns—namely, through bribes, contract concessions, patronage, and other deal making with billionaire private and state contractors. The Center-Left imagined it could compete with the free-market right wing in financing campaigns and candidates via swindlers—and not through class struggle. This was a game they could never master.

The Right, however, mobilized their allies within police, judicial and public institutions to prosecute and disqualify the Center-Left for committing the same crimes for which the Right had evaded prosecution.

The Center-Left did not mobilize the workers and employees to establish even minimal controls over the elite or to assume some managerial power. They thought they could compete with the Right on its own terms, through shady business and chicanery.

The Center-Left relied on financing its administration and policies through the commodity boom in demand for its natural resources, overlooking the fundamental instability and volatility of the global commodity market. While the Right openly condemned the weakness of the Center-Left, in private, it pursued policies even more dependent on overseas speculators and narrow elites.

In Argentina, as the economy declined, the leadership of the right wing, led by Mauricio Macri, launched a successful presidential campaign involving the mass media, banks, middle class voters, and agro-mining elites. Immediately upon taking power, the Macri regime cut social services for workers and the lower middle class, slashing their living standards and laying off thousands of government employees. Obama saw Macri as his kind of legacy savior and viewed Argentina as the new center of US power in Latin America, while implementing plans for more regime change in Brazil, Venezuela and throughout the region.

In Brazil, the center-left Workers' Party (PT) faced a massive attack on its power base by the extreme right wing parties. Corruption scandals rocked the entire spectrum of the political class, but the PT was most heavily implicated by massive fraud in Brazil's huge national oil company, Petrobras. The PT regime's troubles intensified as the country entered a recession with the drop in demand for its agro-mining exports. Growing fiscal deficits compounded the regime's problems. The Brazilian hard Right mobilized its entire apparatus of elite power—the courts, judges, police and intelligence agencies—in a bid to overthrow the PT government and impose an authoritarian neoliberal regime, seizing all financial, business and productive assets

The Center-Left had never been very left, if at all. Under Presidents Lula and Rousseff (2003-2016), the powerful mining and agricultural elites flourished; banking, investment and multi-national enterprises prospered. The Center-Left made some paternalistic concessions to the lowest income classes, and increased wages for labor and farm workers. But the PT relegated labor to the background while it signed business agreements and granted tax concessions to capital. It failed to engage Brazilian workers in class struggle.

The Right was never engaged in any struggle with a genuine leftist government pressing business for structural changes. Nevertheless, the Right sought to eliminates even the most superficial reforms. It would accept nothing short of total control, including the privatization of the major national oil company, the reduction of wages, pensions and transport subsidies, and a slashing of social programs. The Brazilian right wing coup—a fake impeachment organized by indicted crooks—is designed to vastly re-concentrate wealth, and re-establish the power of business, while plunging millions into poverty and repressing the principal organized mass movements. In Brazil, the elite-controlled media, courts and politicians act as judge, jury and jailers against a center-left regime which had never taken control over the major institutions of elite power.

Obama and the Axis of his Legacy

Political rightists join police to control the multitudes and seize power, re-establishing deep ties among Brazil, Washington and Argentina. They will then move toward the neoliberal re-conquest of all Latin America. Against this new wave, it must be understood that Obama's Latin American legacy is too recent, too hasty and too disjointed—the new Right exhibits the same or even worse features of the recently deceased Left.

Argentina's Macri borrows $15 Billion at 8% interest, when the economy is fracturing, employment is collapsing, exports and worldwide demand is declining. At the same time, President Mauricio Macri's cabinet is plagued by major financial scandals a la Panama Papers. The entire political party-trade union-employed working class is profoundly disenchanted with Macri's minority rule.

Argentina may not turn out to be Obama's enduring Latin legacy. While Macri may open the door for a brief Washington take-over, the results will be catastrophic and the future, given Argentina's recent history of popular street uprisings, is uncertain.

Likewise in Brazil, the impeachment/coup has resulted in new and more numerous investigations with trials of post-impeachment politicians and a deepening economic crisis. Brazil's Vice-President, who turned against Rousseff, now faces corruption charges, as do his supporters. The prolonged confrontation precludes any basic continuity. The right wing regime's policy of slashing wages, pensions and poverty 'baskets' will detonate large-scale confrontations with the polarized population. Obama's legacy will be a brief episode, celebrating the ouster of the Workers' Party President followed by a long period of instability and disorder.

Rightist regimes in Venezuela, Colombia and Peru will be part of Obama's legacy but to what lasting end?

The Venezuelan right wing congress, dubbed the MUD, seeks to overthrow the elected president. It demands the release of several right-wing assassins from prison, the privatization of the oil industry, and a deep cut in social programs (health and education). It would reduce employees' wages and eliminate food subsidies. The MUD has no competent plan or capacity to grow the oil economy and overcome chronic food shortages. The MUD would merely replace the Left's subsidized economy with massive price increases for basic commodities, reducing domestic consumption to a fraction of its current level. In other words, the right-wing offensive may defeat the Chavista left but it will not stabilize Venezuela or develop a viable neoliberal alternative. Any new right wing regime will deteriorate rapidly and the chronic problem of criminal violence will exceed the current levels. The alliance between Washington and Venezuela's far right will hardly support Obama's claim to a historic legacy. More likely, it will serve as another example of a failed right wing state unable to replace a weakening left regime.

Similar circumstances can be found among other 'emerging' rightist regimes.

In Colombia, the current right wing President Santos talks to the FARC guerrillas, but also accommodates the paramilitary death squads. His talks of peace settlements and social reform are linked to the genocidal right, led by the former President Uribe. Meanwhile, the economy stagnates with oil and metal prices collapsing on the world market. Colombian living standards have declined and the promise of a right wing revival grows dim. The US-Colombian alliance may undercut the FARC but the right wing does not offer any prospect for modernizing the economy or stabilizing the society.

Similarly in Peru, the right wing wins votes and embraces free markets, but growth declines, investments and profits dry up and mass disenchantment grows among the poor, promising to lead to street conflicts.

The Obama legacy in Latin America has followed

a series of brutal victories, which have no capacity to re-impose a stable new order of free markets and free elections. The initial wave of favorable investments and lucrative concessions will fail to revive the economy and recalibrate a new growth dynamics.

More ominously, Obama relied on mass murder to replace an elected leftist-nationalist president in Honduras, and imposed a regime of terror against the poor and indigenous population. Meanwhile, illicit offshore handouts reward speculators in Argentina.

Obama's legacy in Latin America reflects an entire spectrum from illicit-right wing coups to oust the elected governments in Brazil and Venezuela, to elected authoritarian presidents in Peru and Colombia with historic links to death squads and multi-million dollar overseas accounts.

Obama's contemporary Latin American legacy reeks of gross electoral manipulation preparing the ground for bloody class wars.

Obama's Legacy in the Ukraine, Yemen and Syria

The Obama regime thought it could manage widespread conflicts, uprisings and wars to advance its global supremacy.

To that end, Obama spent billions of dollars in weapons and propaganda arming Neo-Nazi para-military troops to seize power in Ukraine. A grotesque, brutal gang of oligarchs (and disgraced, foreign fugitives like the ousted Georgian leader, Mikhail Saakashvili) served Washington in the puppet Kiev regime. Critics, journalists, jurists, and citizens are being assassinated. The economy has collapsed; prices skyrocket, incomes declined by half, unemployment tripled, and millions have sought refuge abroad. Wars raged between Russian ethnic citizen armies in the Donbass and the puppet Kiev regime. The people of Crimea voted to rejoin Russia. Meanwhile, economic sanctions against trade with Russia have exacerbated shortages for the people of Ukraine.

Under Obama's stewardship the Ukraine became a world-class ... basket case: so much for his European legacy. He can rightly claim credit for imposing a thoroughly retrograde regime of klepto-capitalism with no redeeming features.

Obama embraced Saudi Arabia's war against Yemen, destroying the life and cities of the poorest nation in the Middle East. Obama's legacy in Yemen stands for the systematic obliteration of a sovereign people. Obama performs his tricks for billionaire Saudi despots while savaging the innocent. Obama pays homage to the Israelis in Palestine and the Saudis in Yemen, the criminals responsible for millions of shattered lives.

What of the Obama legacy in Syria and Libya? How many million Africans and Arabs have been murdered or fled on rotten boats in destitution? Only the rankest gang of corrupt media pundits in the US media can pretend this gangster president should evade a war crimes tribunal. His legacy in Iran has yet to prove itself as trade sanctions and military encirclement remain in place.

Conclusion

The Obama regime has pursued wars of unremitting destruction. It has forged partnerships with terrorists and death squads as it seeks short-term imperial victories, which end in dismal failures.

The imperial legacy of this 'historic' president is a mirage of pillage, squalor and destruction. The effect of his political lies has even begun register among the American public: Who trusts the US Congress and the President? And in Europe, who trusts Obama's European partners as they eagerly pushed for wars in the Middle East and North Africa and now fear and loathe the millions of their victims—refugees fleeing to the cities of Europe, with the drowned corpses of uprooted communities despoiling their beaches?

Obama pushed for wars and the Europeans receive the victims with fear and disgust.

Obama's victories are temporary, blighted, and reversed or likely to be.

Obama bombed Afghanistan yesterday and now flees renewed resistance.

Obama's allies are again plundering Latin America but face imminent ouster via popular uprisings.

Obama terrorized and fragmented Syria yesterday but lost Syrian elections the day after.

Obama threatens China's economy while the US continues to eagerly buy China's products.

The Obama legacy began as a failed military and economic offensive accompanying a profound social crisis. During his final year in office, Obama tries to forge alliances with the dregs of the hard right to save his legacy. His brief advance into this sordid world of neoliberals, neo-Nazis and Saudi despots is a prelude to more retreat and chaos.

Obama's public celebration of the right turn in Asia, Latin America, Europe and the Middle East applauds the most retrograde alignment of forces in modern times: Saudis and Israelis; Egyptian generals and Libyan jihadis; neo-Ottoman Turks with Ukrainian gangster-oligarchs. Regime changes in Argentina and Brazil encourage Obama to claim vindication of his imperial legacy.

His 'moment' of imperial truth is brief, all too brief. Everywhere, we witness the rapid rise of imperial success followed by a series of debacles.

Throughout Latin America capitalist profiteers plunge into wild financial adventures, theft and chaos. In the Middle East, the US stands on the crumbling palaces of a moribund Saudi regime. The much-proclaimed imperial advances are based on grand theft everywhere, from Egypt and Turkey to the Ukraine.

Simply stated: the US formula for a successful legacy is failing at the precise moment that it claims success! Obama and the Right have created a world of chaos and disintegration. Obama and his legions, the US, and Europe have no future in peace or war, election or defeats.

There is no imperial legacy for the 'historic' President Obama!

| Chapter Nine |

GLOBAL ECONOMIC, POLITICAL AND MILITARY CONFIGURATIONS

Introduction

Mapping the emerging global economic, political and military configurations requires that we examine regions and countries along several dynamic policy axes:
1. Capitalist versus anti-capitalist
2. Neoliberal versus anti-neoliberal
3. Austerity versus anti-austerity
4. War command centers and war zones
5. Political change and socio-economic continuity
6. New Order and political decay

Though many of these dimensions overlap, they also highlight the complexity and influence of local and national versus global power relations.

We will first identify and classify the regimes and emerging movements, which fall into each of these categories, and then proceed to generalize about current 'global' trends and future perspectives based on approximations of the real correlation of forces.

Capitalism versus Anti-Capitalism

Capitalism is the only economic system throughout the world. However, it has and continues to experience periods of severe crisis, stagnation, and breakdown. Several regimes continue to declare themselves 'socialist' (like Cuba, Venezuela and China) even as they pursue large scale foreign investments, establish free trade zones, and provide incentives to stimulate expansion of the private sector.

Anti-capitalist parties, movements and trade unions have emerged and some still engage in large-scale class struggles. But others have capitulated, like Syriza in Greece, and Refundacion Comunista in Italy, which have renounced any anti-capitalist pretense and embraced neoliberal variants of capitalism.

Anti-capitalist tendencies are at best implicit in the mass working class strikes occurring in China, India, and South Africa, and explicitly by minor parties in Europe, Asia, South America, and elsewhere. Much more significant are the conflicts and struggles between variants of capitalism: neoliberal and anti-neoliberal regimes and movements; and between austerity and anti-austerity regimes and movements.

In military terms, conflicts can best be understood by differentiating between war (command) centers in the imperial countries and war zones.

Neoliberal and Anti-Neoliberal Correlations of Power

The balance of power has shifted toward pro-neoliberal regimes over the past two years. Even where political regime changes have occurred, they have not been accompanied by any significant shifts toward anti-neoliberal policies.

Latin America has witnessed the biggest shift

toward hard-right neoliberal regimes and policies. Right wing extremists won presidential elections in Argentina and legislative elections in Venezuela. In Brazil the so-called 'Workers' Party' regime has embraced a neoliberal austerity program. In Bolivia, the social democratic Movement to Socialism lost the recent referendum to allow a 3rd term re-election for President Evo Morales. The organized forces that defeated the referendum were predominantly hardline neoliberals. Elsewhere in Latin America political changes, from hardline neoliberal presidents to ostensible social democrats (Chile and El Salvador) and nationalists (Peru), simply led to the continuation of free market economic policies. Even socialist regimes, like Cuba, have introduced market incentives and free trade zones for foreign multi-nationals.

In the Middle East and North Africa, popular revolts against incumbent neoliberal despots were violently suppressed. Recycled neoliberal military autocrats and politicians returned to power in Egypt, Tunisia, Israel, Iraq and Yemen.

Iran, under the recently elected 'reformist' Rohani regime, has opened the oil and gas fields to foreign capital and captured about 40% of the legislative deputies in the February 2016 election.

In Asia, neoliberals, who took power in recent elections in India and Indonesia, are moving to de-regulate and promote foreign multinational capital penetration. China and Russia moved to facilitate financial capital flows, resulting in multi-billion-dollar capital flight and the relocation of new billionaire families to Canada, England, the US and other Western countries.

In Europe, Scandinavian and the Low Countries, Social Democrats have embraced and deepened neoliberal policies even as they lose support to right wing anti-immigrant parties.

In the Baltic states of Estonia, Latvia, and Lithuania hardline neoliberals have imposed harsh austerity programs provoking protests of no great political consequence, as the opposition has promoted the same policies.

Russia, under Putin, has succeeded in the reconstruction of the state and economy after the destructive policies of Gorbachev and Yeltsin. But apart from ending the flagrant pillage of the economy by a gangster-ridden oligarchy, Russia is still an oil-dependent state in which billionaires invest and disinvest with facility.

Greece, which became a bankrupt vassal state under the rule of corrupt right wing parties, experienced an electoral revolt in January of 2015, electing a supposedly leftist "anti-neoliberal" party. Syriza, under the leadership of Alexander Tsipras, embraced a brutal European Union–IMF austerity program, plunging Greece deeper into debt, stagnation, poverty, and vassalage.

In Portugal, an anti-austerity alliance between the Socialist (social democrats) and the Communist and Left Bloc parties formed a new government. However, under pressure from the EU, it capitulated, surrendering its tepid anti-austerity proposals.

In Canada, the opposition Liberal Party defeated the Conservatives, offering cosmetic changes and promptly reneging on its promises to end austerity.

In sum, the neoliberal-austerity onslaught provoked mass electoral opposition that led to political changes, bringing to power parties and leaders who embraced almost identical policies! In some cases, the changes deepened neoliberal policies by extending austerity measures; in other cases, they modified some of the restrictions on salaries and social expenditures.

The February (2016) elections in Ireland are a case in point: The neoliberal austerity enthusiasts in the governing coalition (Fine Gael and the Labor Party) were defeated and the Fianna Fáil re-emerged as a leading party, even though it had brought about the economic crisis and breakdown! The only exception to this revolving door politics was an increase in the vote for the national-populist Sinn Fein Party and a scattering of anti-neoliberal and left parties. In the end, the two neoliberal parties are likely to form a coalition regime.

In Europe, the main anti-neoliberal, anti-austerity parties are right wing conservatives who have won election in Poland and Hungary, and opposition parties like the National Front in France.

The major exception is in Spain where a leftist party, Podemos, has embraced an anti-austerity program, even as it offered to form a coalition government with the neoliberal Socialist Party. The coalition regime never came about.

The return, continuation and triumph of neoliberal and austerity parties and policies occur despite a deepening economic crisis and growing popular hostility.

In the Middle East, North Africa, the Baltic and Eastern European states, Egypt, Tunisia, Lithuania, and Poland, repression has undercut leftist opposition.

Nationalist parties and conservative regimes have pre-empted attacks on austerity as is the case in France and Hungary and have marginalized the Left.

International tensions, wars, coups and military build-ups in Ukraine, Syria, Yemen, Turkey, and Southeast Asia have temporarily undercut popular opposition to neoliberal and austerity programs.

In the Ukraine, the US-backed neoliberal regime has virtually collapsed and is widely discredited. The problem is that the most aggressive opposition comes from the neo-Nazi Right!

In the short-run, international conflicts have temporarily distracted popular opposition to neoliberalism. However, over time, the wars, coups and military destruction are exacerbating the domestic crisis, as refugees flood and threaten to disintegrate the European Union.

EU sanctions toward Russia over the Ukraine exacerbated the economic crisis.

The Saudi-Turkey-US-EU-sponsored terror war against Syria and its allies heightens tensions and dampens investment in the region.

In other words, neoliberal-austerity regimes are threatened less by internal opposition than they are by the expansion of war zones, emanating from imperial war centers.

War Centers and War Zones

The economic and political configurations and divisions we have described emphasize the varieties of capitalist regimes, the advance of neoliberalism and the emergence of variations among capitalists (austerity versus anti-austerity). US and EU militarism has deepened cleavages between emergent (China) and re-emergent (Russia) capitalist powers.

The political-economic map and the correlation of forces are deeply affected by military conflicts.

Wars, coups and insurgencies profoundly impact the scope, depth and character of socio-economic systems, above and beyond the dichotomies stated above.

Essentially the global military divisions can be understood through identifying war (imperial command) centers and war zones.

War centers (US, EU) are countries and regimes, which plan, organize, fund and execute military action against other countries. The war centers usually are run by imperialist regimes, which span the globe with military bases in order to defend and promote financial and multinational corporation domination in other countries.

The war centers form alliances, but also compete among themselves; they have follower regimes providing bases, mercenary soldiers and political support, even to the point of sacrificing their own economic goals in order to serve the dominant war centers. Follower regimes participate only at the periphery of decision-making.

War centers have global interests (US, EU), regional interests (Saudi Arabia and Israel—the Middle East) and local interests (Ukraine—Crimea).

The war centers with global interests have clearly defined adversaries: They target emerging military and economic competitors, like Russia and China; nationalist regimes, like Venezuela, Syria and Iran; popular anti-imperialist movements (Hezbollah in Lebanon) and Islamist anti-Western movements (Taliban in Afghanistan). The war centers, at the same time, correlate with neoliberal regimes and destroy or undermine lucrative markets and prosperous sites for investments by expanding the war zones.

War zones, defined by the US and the EU, have included Iraq, Syria, Afghanistan, Libya, Somalia, Ukraine and earlier Yugoslavia. The ensuing wars succeeded in ousting incumbent regimes and splintering target countries, but failed to consolidate political control and, above all, have destroyed hundreds of billions of dollars in investment, trade, financial and resource extraction opportunities.

The war centers have engaged in three levels of military engagement: (1) High intensity, signifying long-term large-scale warfare involving massive expenditures and commitments of troops such as in Iraq and Afghanistan; (2) Middle level intensity, involving US-EU air wars and the use of proxy mercenaries as in Syria, Ukraine and Libya; and (3)

Low intensity wars providing military support to regional allies, e.g. Israel's onslaughts against the Palestinians, Saudi Arabia's assault on Yemen and Turkey's war against the Kurds in Iraq, Syria and Kurdish regions of Turkey.

The war centers in the EU and US have differences over China. The EU favors market expansion, while the US seeks to intensify the military encirclement of China.

Likewise, Europe and the US have differences over sanctions against Russia: the economic elite in the European Union, with billions of Euros invested in Russia, is divided. Meanwhile the US mobilizes its clients in Poland, Romania, and the Baltic countries to escalate military operations on Russia's borders.

The growth of military tensions reflects both economic competition (US-EU versus China) and military expansion (US-EU coups in Ukraine).

Conclusion

The growth and advance of neoliberal and austerity regimes are largely the outcome of domestic or internal class conflicts. These, in turn, are the result of political-electoral contests where the imperial powers play an indirect role (mostly financial/propaganda).

In other words, the advance of neoliberal capitalism is not a result of imperial wars. Neoliberal capitalism conquers because of its electoral advances and because of the defeats, retreats and capitulations of the trade unions and leftist political parties.

The limits of neoliberalism have been clearly set by destructive wars from the imperial military centers; the sanctions imposed on independent capitalist countries; and the alliances with destructive, aspiring regional hegemons (Israel, Turkey and Saudi Arabia).

The prolonged war economy and the neoliberal policies of the imperial centers have concentrated wealth, undermined economic growth, provoked downward social mobility and led to massive population displacement in war zones.

Widespread malaise among voters subject to the destabilization and disintegration of the European Union and the brutal concentration of wealth, power and privilege within the US has led to the emergence of social democratic and right wing nationalist mass electoral movements.

High intensity warfare and prolonged austerity and social polarization have created a chaotic political universe and a multitude of diverse conflicts within the capitalist system.

If the anti-capitalist left is nowhere near overthrowing the system, the system may self-destruct, in a war of all against all: the great sow devouring her own progeny.

| Chapter Ten |

THE INTERNATIONAL MONETARY FUND'S ROGUES' GALLERY

Introduction

The IMF is the leading international monetary agency whose public purpose is to maintain the stability of the global financial system through loans linked to proposals designed to enhance economic recovery and growth.

In fact, the IMF has been under the control of the US and Western European states, and its policies have been designed to further the expansion, domination and profits of their leading multinational corporations and financial institutions.

The US and European states practice a division of powers: the executive directors of the IMF are Europeans; their counterparts in the World Bank (WB) are from the US. The executive directors of the IMF and WB operate in close consultation with US and European governments and especially their Treasury Departments in deciding priorities, deciding what countries will receive loans, under what terms, and how much.

The loans and terms set by the IMF are closely coordinated with the private banking system. Once the IMF signs an agreement with a debtor country, it is a signal for the big private banks to lend, invest, and proceed with a multiplicity of favorable financial transactions. From the above it can be deduced that the IMF plays the role of general command for the global financial system.

The IMF lays the groundwork for the major banks' conquest of the financial systems of the world's vulnerable states. The IMF assumes the burden of doing all the dirty work through its intervention. This includes the usurpation of sovereignty, the demand for privatization and reduction of social expenditures, salaries, wages and pensions, as well as ensuring the priority of debt payments. The IMF acts as the 'blind' for the big banks by deflecting political critics and social unrest.

Executive Directors as Hatchet Persons

What kind of persons do the banks support as executive directors of the IMF? Who do they entrust with the task of violating the sovereign rights of a country, impoverishing its people, and eroding its democratic institutions?

The entrusted persons have included a convicted financial swindler; a person facing prosecution on charges of mishandling public funds as a finance minister; a rapist; an advocate of gunboat diplomacy and the promotor of the biggest financial collapse in a country's history.

IMF Executive Directors on Trial

The current executive director of the IMF (July 2011-2015), Christine Lagarde, is on trial in France for misappropriation of a $400-million-dollar payoff to tycoon

Bernard Tapie while she was Finance Minister in the government of President Sarkozy.

The previous executive director (November 2007-May 2011), Dominique Strauss-Kahn, was forced to resign after he was charged with raping a chambermaid in a New York hotel, and was later arrested and tried for pimping in the city of Lille, France.

His predecessor, Rodrigo Rato (June 2004-October 2007), was a Spanish banker who was arrested and charged with tax evasion, for concealing 27 million euros in seventy overseas banks and swindling thousands of small investors whom he convinced to put their money in a Spanish bank, Bankia, that went bankrupt.

His predecessor, German Horst Kohler (2000-2004), resigned from the German presidency in 2010 after he stated an unlikely verity—namely that overseas military intervention was necessary to defend German economic interests, such as free trade routes.

Michel Camdessus (January 1987-February 2000) was the author of the "Washington Consensus" doctrine that underwrote the global neoliberal counter-revolution. His term of office witnessed his embrace and financing of some of the worst dictators of the time, including his own photo-ops with Indonesian strongman and mass murderer, General Suharto. Under Camdessus, the IMF collaborated with Argentine President Carlos Menem in liberalizing the economy, deregulating financial markets, and privatizing over a thousand enterprises. The crisis which ensued led to the worst depression in Argentine history, with over 20,000 bankruptcies, 25% unemployment, and poverty rates exceeding 50% in working class districts ... Camdessus later regretted his "policy mistakes" with regard to the Argentine's collapse. He was never arrested or charged with crimes against humanity.

Conclusion

The criminal behavior of the IMF executives is not an anomaly or hindrance to their selection. On the contrary, they were selected because they reflect the values, interests, and behavior of the global financial elite: Swindles, tax evasion, bribery, and large-scale transfers of public wealth to private accounts are the norm for the financial establishment. These qualities fit the needs of bankers who have confidence in dealing with their 'mirror-image' counterparts in the IMF.

The international financial elite needs IMF executives who have no qualms in using double standards and who overlook gross violations of its standard procedures. For example, the current executive director, Christine Lagarde, lends $30 billion to the puppet regime in the Ukraine, even though the financial press describes in great detail how corrupt oligarchs have stolen billions with the complicity of the political class.[1] The same Lagarde changes the rules on debt repayment allowing the Ukraine to default on its payment of its sovereign debt to Russia. The same Lagarde insists that the center-right Greek government further reduce pensions in Greece below the poverty level, provoking the otherwise accommodating regime of Alexis Tsipras to call for the IMF to stay out of the bailout.[2]

Clearly the savage cuts in living standards, which the IMF executives decree everywhere, is not unrelated to their felonious personal history. Rapists, swindlers, militarists, are just the right people to direct an institution as it impoverishes the 99% and enriches the 1% of the super-rich.

Endnotes

1 *Financial Times*, 12/21/15, pg. 7.
2 *Financial Times*, 12/21/15, pg.1.

| Chapter Eleven |

WARS: US MILITARIST FACTIONS IN COMMAND

Introduction

Over the past 15 years the US has been engaged in a series of wars, which has led many writers to refer to as the 'rise of militarism'—the growth of an empire, built primarily by and for the projection of military power—and only secondarily to advance economic imperialism.

The rise of a military-based empire, however, does not preclude the emergence of competing, conflicting, and convergent power configurations within the imperial state. These factions of the Washington elite define the objectives and targets of imperial warfare, often on their own terms.

Having stated the obvious general fact of the power of militarism within the imperial state, it is necessary to recognize that the key policymakers, who direct the wars and military policy, will vary according to the country targeted, type of warfare engaged in, and their conception of the war. In other words, while US policy is imperialist and highly militaristic, the key policymakers, their approach, and the outcomes of their policies will differ. There is no fixed strategy devised by a cohesive Washington policy elite guided by a unified strategic vision of the US Empire.

In order to understand the current, seemingly endless wars, we have to examine the shifting coalitions of the elites who make the decisions in Washington but not always primarily for Washington. Some factions of the policy elite have clear conceptions of the American empire, but others improvise and rely on superior political or lobbying power to successfully push their agenda in the face of repeated failures and suffer no consequences or costs.

We will start by listing US imperial wars during the last decade and a half. We will then identify the main policymaking faction which has been the driving force in each war. We will discuss their successes and failures as imperial policymakers and conclude with an evaluation of "the state of the empire" and its future.

Imperial Wars: From 2001–2015

The current war cycle started in late 2001 with the US invasion and occupation of Afghanistan. This was followed by the invasion and occupation of Iraq in March 2003, the US arms support for Israel's invasion of Lebanon in 2006, the proxy invasion of Somalia in 2006/7; the massive re-escalation of war in Iraq and Afghanistan in 2007–2009; the bombing, invasion and regime change in Libya in 2011; the ongoing proxy-mercenary war against Syria (since 2012), and the ongoing 2015 Saudi-US invasion and destruction of Yemen. In Europe, the US was behind the 2014 proxy putsch and violent regime change in Ukraine which has led to an ongoing war against ethnic Russian speakers in southeast Ukraine, especially the populous industrial heartland of the Donbass region.

Over the past 15 years, there have been overt and covert military interventions, accompanied by an intense, provocative military buildup along Russia's borders in the Baltic States, Eastern Europe (especially Poland), the Balkans (Bulgaria and Romania) and at the mammoth US base in Kosovo; in Central Europe with nuclear missiles in Germany and, of course, the annexation of Ukraine and Georgia as US-NATO clients.

Parallel to the military provocations encircling Russia, Washington has launched a major military, political, economic, and diplomatic offensive aimed at isolating China and affirming US supremacy in the Pacific.

In South America, US military intervention found expression via Washington-orchestrated business-military coup attempts in Venezuela in 2002 and Bolivia in 2008, and a successful regime change in Honduras in 2009, overthrowing its elected president and installing a US puppet.

In summary, the US has been engaged in three or more wars since 2001, defining an almost exclusively militarist empire, run by an imperial state directed by civilian and military officials seeking unchallenged global dominance through violence.

Washington: Military Workshop of the World

War and violent regime change are the exclusive means through which the US now advances its foreign policy. However, the various Washington war-makers among the power elite do not form a unified bloc with common priorities. Washington provides the weapons, soldiers, and financing for whichever power configuration or faction among the elite is in a position, by design or default, to seize the initiative and push forward their own war agenda.

The invasion of Afghanistan was significant insofar

as it was seen by all sectors of the militarist elite as the first in a series of wars. Afghanistan was to set the stage for the launching of higher priority wars elsewhere.

Afghanistan was followed by the infamous 'Axis of Evil' speech, dictated by Tel Aviv, penned by presidential speech-writer David Frum and mouthed by the brainless President Bush, II. The 'Global War on Terror' was the thinly veiled slogan for serial wars around the world. Washington made it clear that it measured the loyalty of its vassals among the nations of Europe, Asia, Africa and Latin America by their support for the invasion and occupation of Afghanistan. The Afghan invasion provided the template for future wars. It led to an unprecedented increase in the military budget and ushered in Caesar-like dictatorial presidential powers to order and execute wars, silencing domestic critics and sending scored of thousands of US and NATO troops to Afghanistan.

In itself, Afghanistan was never any threat and certainly no economic prize for plunder and profit. The Taliban had not attacked the US. Osama Bin Laden could have been turned over to a judicial tribunal—as the then-governing Taliban had insisted.

The US military (with its 'Coalition of the Willing' or COW) successfully invaded and occupied Afghanistan, and set up a vassal regime in Kabul. It built scores of military bases and attempted to form an obedient colonial army. In the meantime, the Washington militarist elite had moved on to bigger and, for the Israel-centric pro-Zionist elite, higher priority wars, namely Iraq.

The decision to invade Afghanistan was not opposed by any of Washington's militarist elite factions. They all shared the idea of using a successful military blitz or 'cake-walk' against the abysmally impoverished Afghanistan as a way to rabble rouse the American masses into accepting a long period of intense and costly global warfare throughout the world.

Washington's militarist elites fabricated the link between the 9/11 attacks, Afghanistan's governing Taliban, and the presence of the Saudi jihadist, Osama Bin Laden. Despite the 'fact' that most of the hijackers were from the kingdom of Saudi Arabia and none were Afghans, invading and destroying Afghanistan was to be the initial test to gauge the highly manipulated and frightened American public's willingness to shoulder the burden of a huge new cycle of imperial wars. This has been the only aspect of the invasion of Afghanistan that could be viewed as a policy success—it made the costs of endless wars acceptable to a relentlessly propagandized public.

Flush with their military and public relations victories in Afghanistan, the Washington militarists turned to Iraq and fabricated a series of increasingly preposterous pretexts for war—linking the purported 9/11 'jihadi' hijackers with the secular regime of Saddam Hussein, whose intolerance for violent Islamists (especially the Saudi variety) was well documented, and concocting a whole fabric of lies about Iraqi weapons of mass destruction, which provided the propaganda basis for invading an already disarmed, blockaded, bombed, and starved Iraq in March 2003.

Zionists, including Paul Wolfowitz, Elliot Abrams, Richard Perle, and a few Israel-centric Gentile militarists, such as Vice President Cheney, Secretary of State Colin Powell and Defense Secretary Rumsfeld led the Washington militarists in designing the war to destroy Iraq. The Zionists had a powerful entourage in key positions in the State Department, Treasury and the Pentagon.

While there were outsiders—non-Zionists and militarists within these institutions, especially the Pentagon, who voiced reservations—they were brushed aside, not consulted and encouraged to retire.

None of the old hands in the State Department or

Pentagon bought into the hysteria about Saddam Hussein's weapons of mass destruction, but to voice their reservations was to risk their career. The manufacture and dissemination of the pretext for invading Iraq was orchestrated by a small team of operatives linking Tel Aviv and Deputy Secretary of Defense Paul Wolfowitz's "Office of Special Plans", a tight group of Zionists and some Israelis headed by Abram Shulsky (Sept. 2002–June 2003).

The US war on Iraq was an important part of Israel's agenda to re-make the Middle East, to establish its unchallenged regional hegemony, and execute a 'final solution' for its vexing Arab (native Palestinian) problem: It was made operational by the powerful Zionist faction within the Executive (White House), which had assumed almost dictatorial powers after the attack on 9/11. Zionists planned the war, designed the occupation policy, and succeeded wildly with the eventual dismemberment of a once-modern, secular, nationalist Arab state.

In order to smash the Iraqi state, the US occupation policy was to eliminate (through mass firings, jailing and assassination) all high level, experienced Iraqi civil, military and scientific personnel, down to high school principals. They dismantled any vital infrastructure, which had not been already destroyed by the decades of US sanctions and bombing under President Clinton, and reduced an agriculturally advanced Iraq to a barren wasteland which would take centuries to recover and could never challenge Israel's colonization of Palestine, let alone its military supremacy in the Middle East. The large Palestinian Diaspora refugee population in Iraq was targeted for special treatment.

But Zionist policymakers had a much larger agenda than erasing Iraq as a viable country. They had a longer list of targets: Syria, Iran, Lebanon and Libya, whose destructions were to be carried out with US and NATO blood and treasure (and not a single Israeli soldier).

Despite the fact that Iraq did not even possess a functioning air force or navy in March 2003 and that Afghanistan in late 2001 was rather primitive, the invasions of both countries turned out to be very costly to the US. The US completely failed to benefit from its victory and occupation, despite Paul Wolfowitz's boasts that the pillage of Iraq's oil fields would pay for the entire project in a few months. This was because the real Zionist plan was to destroy these nations beyond any possibility for a quick or cheap imperialist economic gain. Scorching the earth and salting the fields is not a very profitable policy for empire builders.

Israel has been the biggest winner, at no cost to the 'Jewish State'. The American Zionist policy elite literally handed Israel the services of the largest and richest armed forces in history: those of the US. Israel-Firsters played a decisive role among Washington policymakers and people in Tel Aviv celebrated in the streets! They came, they dominated policy, and they accomplished their mission: Iraq (and millions of its people) was destroyed.

The US gained an unreliable, broken colony, with a devastated economy, systematically destroyed infrastructure, and lacking the functioning civil service needed for a modern state. To pay for the mess, the American people faced a spiraling budget deficit, tens of thousands of American war casualties and massive cuts in their own social programs. Crowning the Washington war-makers' victory was the disarticulation of American civil and constitutional rights and liberties, and the construction of an enormous domestic police state.

After the Iraq disaster, the same influential Zionist faction in Washington lost no time in demanding a new war against Israel's bigger enemy: Iran. In the ensuing years, they failed to push the US to attack Teheran, though they succeeded in imposing crippling sanctions on Iran. The Zionist faction secured massive US military support for Israel's abortive invasion of Lebanon and its devastating series of blitzkriegs against the impoverished and trapped people of Gaza.

The Zionist faction then successfully shaped US military interventions to meet Israel's regional ambitions against three Arab countries: Yemen, Syria and Libya. The Zionists were not able to manipulate the US into attacking Iran because the traditional militarist faction in Washington balked: With instability in Afghanistan and Iraq, the US was not well positioned to face a major conflagration throughout the Middle East, South Asia and beyond, which a ground and air war with Iran would involve. However, the Zionist factions did secure brutal economic sanctions against Iran and the appointment of key Israel-centric officials within the US Treasury. As Under Secretary for Terrorism and Financial Intelligence, Stuart Levey, at the start of the Obama regime, and David Cohen afterwards, were positioned to enforce the sanctions.

Even before the ascendency of Israeli Prime Minister Binyamin Netanyahu, Tel Aviv's military objectives after Iraq, including Iran, Syria, Lebanon, Libya and Yemen had to be spaced over time, because the non-Zionist factions among Washington's elite had been unable to integrate occupied Afghanistan and Iraq into the empire.

Resistance, armed conflict and military advances in both Afghanistan and Iraq never ceased and are continuing into their second decade. As soon as the US would withdraw from a region, declaring it 'pacified', the armed resistance would move back in and the local sepoys would defect to the rebels or take off for London or Washington with millions in pillaged loot.

Unfinished wars, mounting casualties and spiraling costs, with no end in sight, undermined the agreement between the militarist and the Zionist factions in the Executive branch. However, the massively powerful Zionist presence in the US Congress provided a platform to bray for new and even bigger wars.

Israel's vicious invasion of Lebanon in 2006 was defeated despite receiving massive US arms supplies, a US-funded Iron Dome missile defense system and intelligence assistance. Tel Aviv could not defeat the highly disciplined and motivated Hezbollah fighters in South Lebanon despite resorting to carpet bombing of civilian neighborhoods with millions of banned cluster munitions, and picking off ambulances and churches sheltering refugees.

Libya: A Multi-faction War for the Militarists (Without Big Oil)

The war against Libya was a result of multiple factions among the Washington militarist elite, including the Zionists, coming together with French, English, and German militarists to smash the most modern, secular, independent state in Africa under the leadership of Muammar Gadhafi.

The aerial campaign against the Gadhafi regime had virtually no organized support within Libya with which to reconstruct a viable neo-colonial state ripe for pillage. This was another planned dismemberment of a complex, modern republic, which had been independent of the US Empire.

The war succeeded wildly in shredding Libya's economy, state, and society. It unleashed scores of armed terrorist groups (who appropriated the modern weapons of Gadhafi's army and police), and uprooted two million black contract workers and Libyan citizens of South Saharan origin, forcing them to flee the rampaging racist militias to the refugee camps of Europe. Untold thousands died in rickety boats in the Mediterranean Sea.

The entire war was carried out to the publicly giddy delight of Secretary of State Hillary Clinton and her 'humanitarian interventionist' lieutenants, Susan Rice and Samantha Power, who were utterly ignorant as to who and what the Libyan "opposition" represented. Eventually, even Hillary's own Ambassador to Libya would be slaughtered by ... the same victorious US-backed 'rebels' [sic] in the newly liberated Bengazi!

The Zionist faction destroyed Gadhafi (whose capture, grotesque torture, and murder was filmed and widely disseminated), eliminating another real adversary of Israel and supporter of Palestinian rights. The US militarist faction, which led the war, got nothing positive—not even a secure naval, air or training base—only a dead Ambassador, and millions of desperate refugees flooding Europe. But it did get thousands of trained and armed jihadists for the next target: Syria.

For a while Libya became the main supply-line for Islamist mercenaries and arms to invade Syria and fight the secular nationalist government in Damascus.

Once again the least influential faction in Washington turned out to be the oil and gas industry, which lost lucrative contracts it had already signed with the Gadhafi government. Thousands of highly-trained foreign oil workers were withdrawn. After Iraq, it should have been obvious that these wars were not 'for oil'!

Ukraine: Coups, Wars, and Russia's 'Underbelly'

With the US-orchestrated coup and intervention in Ukraine, the militarist factions once again seized the initiative, establishing a puppet regime in Kiev and targeting

Russia's strategic 'soft underbelly'. The plan had been to take over Russia's strategic military bases in Crimea and cut Russia off from the vital military-industrial complexes in the Donbass region with its vast iron and coal reserves.

The mechanics of the power grab were relatively well planned, the political clients were put in power, but the US militarists had made no contingencies for propping up the Ukrainian economy, once cut loose from its main trading partner and oil and gas supplier, Russia.

The coup led to a proxy war in the ethnic-Russian majority regions in the south east (the Donbass) with four unanticipated consequences: 1) a country divided east and west along ethno-linguistic lines, (2) a bankrupt economy made even worse by the imposition of an IMF austerity program, (3) a corrupt crony capitalist elite, which was pro-West by bank account, and (4) after two years, mass disaffection among voters toward the US puppet regime.

The militarists in Washington and Brussels succeeded in engineering the coup in Ukraine but lacked the domestic allies, plans, and preparations to run the country and successfully annex it to the EU and NATO as a viable country.

Apparently the militarist factions in the State Department and Pentagon are much more proficient in stage managing coups and invasions than in establishing a stable regime thereafter as part of a New World Order. They succeed in the former and fail repeatedly in the latter.

The Pivot to Asia and the Pirouette to Syria

During most of the previous decade, traditional global strategists in Washington increasingly objected to the Zionist faction's domination and direction of US war policies focused on the Middle East for the benefit of Israel, instead of meeting the growing challenge of the new world economic superpower in Asia, China.

US economic supremacy in Asia had been deeply eroded as China's economy grew at double digits. Beijing was displacing the US as the major trading partner in the Latin American and African markets. Meanwhile, the top 500 US MNCs were heavily invested in China. Three years into President Obama's first term the China-militarist faction announced a shift from the Middle East and the Israel-centric agenda to a pivot to Asia, the source of 40% of the world's industrial output.

But it was not profits and markets that motivated Washington's Asia faction among the militarist elites—the motivation was still military power. Even trade agreements, like the Trans Pacific Partnership (TPP), were viewed as tools to encircle and weaken China militarily and undermine its regional influence.

Led by the hysterical Pentagon boss, Ashton Carter, Washington prepared a series of major military confrontations with Beijing off the coast of China.

The US signed expanded military base agreements with the Philippines, Japan and Australia; it participated in military exercises with Vietnam, South Korea and Malaysia; it dispatched battleships and aircraft carriers into Chinese territorial waters.

The US confrontational trade policy was formulated once again by a Zionist trio: Secretary of Commerce, Penny Pritzer; Trade Negotiator Michael Froman (who works for both the Asia militarist and Zionist factions); and Treasury Secretary Jake Lew. The result was the Trans-Pacific Partnership (TPP), involving 12 Pacific countries while deliberating excluding China. Washington's Asian militarist faction planned to militarize the entire Pacific Basin in order to dominate the maritime trade routes and be able, at a moment's notice, to choke off all of China's overseas markets and suppliers—shades of the series of US provocations against Japan leading up to the US entering WW2.

The Asia-militarist faction successfully demanded a bigger military budget to accommodate its vastly more aggressive posture toward China.

Predictably, China has insisted on defending its maritime routes and has increased its naval and air base building, and sea and air patrols. Also predictably, China has countered the US-dominated TPP by setting up a one hundred billion dollar Asia Infrastructure Investment Bank (AIIB), while contributing to the multi-billion dollar BRICS Bank. Meanwhile, China has even signed a separate $30 billion dollar trade agreement with Washington's strategic 'partner', Britain. In fact, Britain followed the rest of the EU and joined the Asia Infrastructure Investment Bank—despite objections from Washington's 'Asia faction'. Notably, as pointed out by analyst Peter Koenig. China and Russia also have developed in the past couple of years their own money transfer system, the China International Payment System, or the CIPS network which replaces the western transfer system, SWIFT, for Russian-Chinese internal trading.[1]

While the US depends heavily on its military pacts with South Korea and Japan, the latter nations have been meeting with China—their most significant trading partner—to work on expanding and deepening economic ties.

Up until 2014, the business-with-China faction of the Washington elite had played a key role in the making of US-Asia policy. However, they have been eclipsed by the Asia-militarist-faction, which is taking US policy in a totally different direction: pushing China out as Asia's economic superpower and escalating military confrontation with Beijing now heads Washington's agenda.

Ashton Carter, the US Defense Secretary, has China, the second most important economy in the world, in the Pentagon's cross-hairs. When the TPP failed to curtail China's expansion, the militarist faction shifted Washington toward a high risk military course, which could destabilize the region and risk a nuclear confrontation.

The Pirouette: China and Syria

Meanwhile in the Levant, Washington's Zionist faction has been busy running a proxy war in Syria. The pivot to Asia has had to compete with the pirouette to Syria and Yemen.

The US joined Saudi Arabia, Turkey, the Gulf Emirates, and the EU in sponsoring a replay of the Libyan regime change—sponsoring proxy terrorists from around the globe into invading and devastating Syria. Damascus has been attacked for varying reasons depending on the interested parties: for posing a secular and multi-ethnic obstacle to the establishment of a regional Sunni Caliphate and for being pro-Palestinian nationalism (the jihadists); for being allied with Shia Iran, Shia Hezbollah, and now Russia, thereby countering US-Israeli regional dominance (the US, Israel, Saudi Arabia); for having an independent foreign policy (the US); and for maintaining a limited representative (but not necessarily democratic) government (the original peaceful Syrian protesters). All parties but the latter would have Syria fractured—something they had accomplished in Iraq and Libya.

But lest we forget, Damascus heretofore, under Assad Sr., was a torture facilitator for the US—and on the other hand, jihadists willing to die for their cause cannot be solely described as mercenaries.

The US militarist faction (personified by Secretary

of Defense Carter and Senators McCain and Graham) have funded, trained and equipped the terrorists, whom they call 'moderates' and had clearly expected their progeny to follow Washington's directions. The emergence of ISIS showed just how closely these 'moderates' stuck to Washington's script. The US is still in search of moderates (or anybody) because they have lost control of ISIS—though they don't necessarily want to take it out, as long as it keeps the conflict going and continues the destruction/pretext for destruction of Syria, which is serving their ends. But the US cannot finish off ISIS only by use of the Kurds.

Initially, the traditional militarist wing of Washington's elite resisted the Zionist faction's demand for direct US military intervention (American 'boots on the ground'). That is changing with recent (very convenient) events in Paris.

From Piecemeal Interventions to Nuclear Confrontation

The Washington militarists continue to commit more US soldiers to Iraq and Afghanistan; American fighter planes and Special Forces are in Syria and Yemen. Meanwhile, US naval armadas aggressively patrol the coasts of China and Iran. The militarist–Zionist 'compromise' over Syria was comprised of an initial contingent of 50 US Special Forces to join in 'limited' combat roles with "loyal" [sic] Islamist mercenaries—the so-called 'moderates'. There are commitments for greater and heavier weaponry to come, including ground to air missiles capable of shooting down Russian and Syrian military jets.

Elite Factional Politics: An Overview

How does the record of these competing factions

formulating US imperial war policies in the Middle East over the past 15 years stack up? Clearly there has been no coherent imperial economic strategy.

The policy toward Afghanistan is remarkable for its failure to end the longest war in US history—over 14 years of occupation! The recent attempts by US-led client NATO forces to withdraw have been immediately followed by military advances by the nationalist-Islamist resistance militia—the Taliban, which controls much of the countryside. The possibility of a collapse of the current puppet in Kabul has forced the militarists in Washington to retain US bases, surrounded by completely hostile rural populations.

The Afghan war's initial appearance of success permitted new wars. But taking the long view, the Afghan war, has been a miserable failure in terms of the stated strategic goal of establishing a stable client government. The Afghan economy has collapsed: opium production (which had been significantly suppressed by the Taliban's poppy eradication campaign in 2000-2001) is the now predominant crop, with cheap heroin flooding Europe and beyond. Under the weight of massive and all-pervasive corruption by 'loyal' client officials, the Afghan treasury is empty. The puppet rulers are totally disconnected from the most important regional, ethnic, religious and family clans and associations.

Washington could not find any viable economic classes in Afghanistan with which to anchor a development strategy. They did not come to terms with the deep ethno-religious consciousness rooted in rural communities, and fought the most popular political force among the majority Pashtu, the Taliban, which had no role in the attack on 9/11.

They artificially slapped together a massive army of surly illiterates under Western imperial command and watched it fall apart at the seams, defect to the Taliban or turn their own guns on the foreign occupation troops. These 'mistakes', which account for the failure of the militarist faction in the Afghanistan war were due, in no small part, to the pressure and influence of the Zionist faction who wanted to quickly move on to their highest priority, a US war against Israel's first priority enemy, Iraq, without consolidating the US control in Afghanistan. For the Zionists, Afghanistan (envisioned as a 'cake-walk' or quick victory) was just a tool to set the stage for a much larger sequence of US wars against Israel's regional Arab and Persian adversaries. Before the militarists could establish any viable order and an enduring governmental structure in Afghanistan, attention shifted to a Zionist-ordained war against Iraq.

The buildup for the US war against Iraq has to be understood as a project wholly engineered by and for the state of Israel, mostly through its agents within the US government and Washington policy elite. The goal was to establish Israel as the unchallenged political-military power in the region using American troops and money, and preparing the ground for Tel Aviv's 'final solution' for the Palestinian 'problem'; massive ... ethnic cleansing and judification.

The US military and occupation campaign included the wholesale and systematic destruction of Iraq: Its law and order, culture, economy, and society—to the extent that there would be no possibility of recovery. Such a vicious campaign did not serve the needs of any productive sector of the US economy (or for that matter, of any Israeli economic interest).

Washington's Zionist faction set about, in a parody of Pol Pot's Khmer Rouge, to identify and destroy any competent, experienced Iraqi professional, civil servant, scientist, intellectual, or military official capable of re-organizing and re-building the county and war-battered society. They were assassinated, arrested, tortured, or driven into exile. The occupation deliberately encouraged religious parties and traditional tribes to engage in inter-communal massacres and ethnic cleansing. In other words, the Zionist faction did not pursue the traditionally understood policy of empire building which would incorporate the second tier functionaries of a conquered state to form a competent client regime and use Iraq's great oil and gas wealth to build its economy, from which the colonial power would benefit. Instead they chose to impose a scorched earth policy; setting loose organized sectarian armies, imposing the rule of grotesquely corrupt ex-pats, and placing the most venal, sectarian clients in positions of power. The effect has been to transform the most advanced, secular Arab country into an 'Afghanistan' and in less than 15 years, destroying centuries of culture and community.

The goal of the Zionist strategy was to destroy Iraq as Israel's regional rival. The cost of million s of Iraqi dead and many million refugees did not prick any conscience in Washington or Tel Aviv. After all, Washington's traditional militarist faction picked up the bill (costing hundreds of billions), which they passed on to the American taxpayers (well over one trillion dollars), and used the deaths and injuries of tens of thousands of American troops as a pretext for spreading more chaos. The result of their mayhem includes the specter of ISIS, which they may consider to be a success, since hysteria over ISIS pushes the West closer to Israel.

The sheer scale of death and destruction inflicted on the Iraqi population by the Zionist faction led to thousands of highly competent Ba'athist officers, who had survived 'Shock and Awe' and the sectarian massacres, to join armed Islamist Sunnis and eventually form the Islamic State in Iraq and Syria (ISIS). This group of experienced Iraqi military officers formed the strategic technical core of Isis, which launched a devastating offensive in Iraq in 2014, taking major cities in the north and completely routing the US-trained puppet armies of the 'government' in Baghdad. From there they moved into Syria and beyond. This is fundamental to understanding the roots of ISIS: The Zionist faction among US militarist policymakers imposed a deliberate 'scorched earth' occupation policy, which united highly-trained nationalist Ba'athist military officers with young Sunni fighters, both locals and increasingly foreign jihadists and mercenaries. These deracinated members of the traditional Iraqi nationalist military elite had lost their families to the US-promoted and facilitated sectarian massacres; they were persecuted, tortured, driven underground, and highly motivated. They literally had nothing left to lose!

This core of the ISIS leadership stands in stark contrast to the colonial, corrupt and demoralized army slapped together by the US military with more cash than morale. ISIS quickly swept through half of Iraq and came within 40 miles of Baghdad.

The US militarist faction faced military defeat after eight years of war. They mobilized, financed, and armed their client Kurdish mercenaries in northern Iraq and recruited the Shia Ayatollah Ali al-Sistani to appeal to the Shia militias.

ISIS exploited the Western-backed Islamist uprising in Syria and extended their sweep well across the border. Syria had accepted a million Iraqi refugees from the US invasion, including many of Iraq's surviving experienced, nationalist, administrative elite. The US militarists are in a dilemma—another full-scale war would not be politically feasible, and its military outcome uncertain ... Moreover the US is aligned with dubious allies—especially the Saudis, who have their own regional ambitions and fears. Turkey, Saudi Arabia, Israel, and the Kurds were each eager to expand their power territorially and politically.

In the midst of this, the traditional Washington

militarists are left with no overall viable imperialist strategy. Instead they improvise with faux 'rebels', who claim to be moderates and democrats while taking US guns and dollars, and ultimately joining the most powerful Islamist groups like Al Qaeda or ISIS.

Throwing a wrench into the machinery of Israeli-Saudi hegemonic ambitions, Russia, Iran, and Hezbollah have sided with the secular Syrian government. Russia finally moved to bomb ISIS strongholds after identifying a significant ISIS contingent of militant Chechens whose ultimate aims are to bring war and terror back to Russia.

The US-EU war against Libya unleashed all the retrograde mercenary forces from three continents (Africa, Asia and Europe) and Washington finds itself with no means to control them. Washington could not even protect its own consulate in their 'liberated' regional capital of Benghazi, where the US ambassador and two intelligence aides were killed by Washington's own 'rebels'. The competing and cooperating factions of the Washington militarist elite placed Libya on a steaming platter, serving up invasion, regicide and hundreds of thousands of refugees, which they did not bother to even season with any plan or strategy—just unadulterated scorched earth against another opponent of Zionism.

As a result, a potentially lucrative, strategic neo-colony in North Africa has been lost with no accountability by the Washington architects for the failure to profit from the engagement, let alone for such acts of barbaric destruction.

Latin America: The Last Outpost of the Multinationals

As we have seen, the major theaters of imperial policy (the Middle East and Asia) have been dominated by civilian militarists, not professional diplomats linked to the

MNCs. Latin America stands as something of an exception. In Latin America, US policymakers have been guided by big business interests. Their main focus has been on pushing the neoliberal agenda. Eventually this has meant promoting the US-centered free trade agreements, joint military exercises, shared military bases, and political backing for the US global military agenda.

The militarist faction in Washington worked with the traditional business faction in support of the unsuccessful military coups in Venezuela (2002 and 2014), the attempted coup in Bolivia 2008, and a successful regime change in Honduras (2010).

To harass the independent Argentine government, which was developing closer diplomatic and trade ties with Iran, a sector of the US Zionist financial elite (the vulture fund magnate, Paul Singer) joined forces with the Zionist militarist faction to raise hysterical accusations against President Cristina Kirchner over the 'mysterious' suicide of a Israel-linked Argentine prosecutor. The prosecutor, Alberto Nisman, had devoted his career to cooking up a case against Iran with the aid of the Mossad and CIA for the unsolved bombing the Buenos Aires Jewish community center in 1994. Various investigations had exonerated Iran from any connection with the death, yet much noise continued to be generated over the "Nisman Affair," in an intense effort to keep Argentina from trading with Iran.

The Washington business faction had operated in a mildly hostile Latin America for most of the past decade. However, it was able to recover influence via a series of bilateral free trade agreements and then took advantage of the downswing of the commodity cycle, which weakened the center-left regimes and moved them closer to Washington.

The excesses committed by the US backed military dictatorships during the nineteen sixties through eighties, and the crisis of the neoliberal nineties, set the stage for the rise of a relatively moderate business-diplomatic faction to come to the fore in Washington, while the various militarist and Zionist factions in Washington were focused elsewhere (Europe, Middle East and Asia). This resulted in the US political elite operating in Latin America mostly via political and business proxies—for the time being.

Conclusion

From our brief survey, it is clear that wars play a key role in US foreign policy in most regions of the world. However, war policies in different regions are driven by different factions in the governing elite.

The traditional militarist faction predominates, creating confrontations in Ukraine, Asia, and along the Russian border. Within that framework the US Army, Air Force, and Special Forces play a leading and fairly conventional role. In the Far East, the Navy and Air Force predominate.

In the Middle East and South Asia, the military (Army and Air Force) factions share power with the Zionist faction. Fundamentally the Zionists dictate policy on Iraq, Lebanon and Palestine, and the militarists follow. Both factions overlapped in creating the debacle in Libya.

The factions form shifting coalitions, supporting wars of interest to their respective power centers. The militarists and Zionists worked together in launching the Afghan war; but once launched, the Zionists abandoned Kabul and concentrated on preparing for the invasion and occupation of Iraq, which was of far greater interest to Israel.

It should be noted that at no point did the oil and business elite play any significant role in war policy. The Zionist faction pushed hard to secure direct US ground intervention in Libya and Syria, but was not able to force the US to send large contingents of ground troops due to opposition from the Russians as well as a growing sector of the US electorate. Likewise, the Zionists played a leading role in successfully imposing sanctions against Iran and a major role in prosecuting banks around the world accused of violating the sanctions. However, they were not able to block the military faction from securing a diplomatic agreement with Iran over its uranium enrichment program without going to war.

Clearly, the business faction plays a major role in promoting US trade agreements and tries to lift or avoid sanctions against important real and potential trade partners like China, Iran, and Cuba.

The Zionist faction among the Washington elite policymakers takes positions which consistently push for wars and aggressive policies against any regime targeted by Israel. The differences between the traditional militarist and Zionist factions are blurred by most writers who scrupulously avoid identifying Zionist decision-makers, but there is no question of who benefits and who loses.

The kind of war which the Zionists promote and implement—the utter destruction of enemy countries—undermines any plans by the traditional militarist faction and the military to consolidate power in an occupied country and incorporate it into a stable empire.

It is a serious error to lump these factions together: the business, Zionist and various militarist factions of the Washington policy making elite are not one homogeneous group. They may overlap at times, but they also differ as to interests, liabilities, ideology and loyalties. They also differ in their institutional allegiances.

The overarching militarist ideology, which permeates US imperial foreign policy, obscures a deep and recurrent weakness: US policymakers master the mechanics of war but have no strategy for ruling after intervening. This has been glaringly evident in all recent wars: Iraq, Syria, Libya, Ukraine, etc. Improvisation has repeatedly led to monumental failures: from financing phantom armies to bleeding billions to prop-up incompetent, kleptocratic puppet regimes. Despite the hundreds of billions of public money wasted in these serial disasters, no policymaker has been held to account.

Long wars and short memories are the norm for Washington's militarist rulers who do not lose sleep over their blunders. The Zionists, for their part, do not even need a strategy for rule. They push the US into wars for Israel, and once having destroyed 'the enemy country' they leave a vacuum to be filled by chaos. The American public provides the gold and blood for these misadventures and reaps nothing but domestic deterioration and greater international strife.

Endnotes

1	Peter Koenig, "The Collapse of the Western Fiat Monetary System may have Begun. China, Russia and the Reemergence of Gold-Backed Currencies," <http://www.globalresearch.ca/the-collapse-of-the-western-fiat-monetary-system-may-have-begun-china-russia-and-the-reemergence-of-gold-backed-currencies/5521107>

| Chapter Twelve |

MANDARIN FOR THE WARLORDS: THE HARVARD SCHOOL OF EMPIRE BUILDING

Introduction

Harvard professor Joseph Nye, a former senior Pentagon functionary, is one of the longest serving and most influential advisers to US empire-building officials. Nye has recently re-affirmed the primacy of the US as a world power in his latest book, *Is the American Century Over?* and his article, "The American Century will survive the Rise of China."[1] These publications are in line with his earlier book, *Bound to Lead,* and his longstanding view that the US is not a declining world power, that it retains 'supremacy' even in the face of China's rise to global power.

Nye's views of US world supremacy have served to encourage Washington to wage multiple wars; his sanguine view of US economic power has allowed policymakers to ignore fundamental weaknesses in the US economy and to overestimate US power, based on the distinctions between what he dubs 'soft' and 'military' power.

In tackling Professor Nye's work, we are not dealing with a detached academic in the ivory tower—we are taking on a high-level political influential, a hardline military hawk, whose views are reflected in the forging of strategic decisions, and whose arguments then serve to justify major government policies.

First, we will proceed through a critical analysis of his theoretical assumptions, historical arguments, and conceptual framework. Then we will consider the political consequences, which have flowed from his analysis and prescriptions. In conclusion, we shall propose an alternative, more realistic, analysis of US global power, one more attuned to the real international position of the US in the world today.

Nye is Ossified in His Distorted Time Warp

Nye's segmentation of power into three spheres— economic, military (hard), and diplomatic/cultural (soft), overlooks the inter-relation between them. What he dubs as 'soft power' usually relies on 'hard power', either before, during or after the application of soft power. Moreover, the capacity to influence by soft power depends on economic promise or military coercion to enforce 'persuasion'. Where economic resources or military threats are not present, soft power is ineffective.

Nye's argument that military power is co-equal with economic power is a very dubious proposition. Over the medium run, economic power buys, expands, and increases military power. In other words, economic resources are convertible into military as well as soft power. It can influence politicians, parties, and regimes via trade, investments, and credit in many ways which military power cannot. Over time, economic power translates into military power. Nye's claims for persisting US military superiority in the face of its admitted economic decline is ephemeral or time bound.

Nye's argument about the continued ascendancy of US global power 'for the next few decades' is a dubious, static view, ignoring a long-term, large-scale, historical trajectory. Lifelong shibboleths never die! By all empirical indicators—economic, political, and even military—the US is a declining power. Moreover, what is important is not where the US is at any given moment but the direction in which it is moving. Its declining shares of Latin American, African, and Asian markets clearly point to a downward trajectory.

Power is a relationship. By definition it means a country's capacity to make other countries or political entities do what they otherwise would not do. To consider the US as the dominant world power, we cannot, as Nye proposes, look at its 'reputation' as a world power or cite its 'military capacity' or willingness to project military force. We need to look at military and political outcomes in multiple key issue areas in which US policymakers have sought to establish regional or local dominance—as would those in other states, equally engaged in assessing US power.

Nye's discussion fails to look at the negative cumulative effects of US policy failures in multiple regions over time in determining whether the US retains its global supremacy or is a declining power. To simply preach that 'the American century is not over', because some critics in the past mistakenly thought that the USSR in the 1970s or Japan in the 1980s would displace the US as the global power, is to overlook the foundational weakness and repeated failures of US policymakers to impose or persuade other nations to accept US supremacy over the past decade and a half.

If, as Nye grudgingly concedes, China has replaced the US as the leading economic power in Asia, he does not understand the dynamic components of Chinese economic power, especially of its long term, large-scale accumulation of foreign reserves and its rapidly growing technical knowhow. Even worse, Nye ignores how the military exercise of world power has actively undermined US economic supremacy.

It is precisely Nye's belief, along with other Pentagon advisers, that it is US military supremacy that makes it a 'world power' that has led to catastrophic, prolonged, and costly wars. These wars have degraded and undermined US pretensions of world leadership or more accurately, imperial supremacy.

While the US has spent trillions of dollars of public money on prolonged and losing wars in Afghanistan, Iraq, and Somalia, as well as on ongoing military interventions in Libya, Syria, Ukraine, and Yemen, China and other emerging powers have engaged in large long-term economic expansion, increasing market shares, acquiring productive enterprises, and expanding their sources of capital accumulation in dynamic regions.

Further and worse, US repeated projections of military power have not created new sources of wealth. The US capacity and willingness to engage in multiple disastrous wars has led to a greater loss of not just military but economic influence.

Consequences of High Military Capacity and Declining Economic Performance

Utilizing its great storehouse of military capacity so disastrously has degraded and weakened the US military as well as its imperial economic reach. Repeated US military defeats, its inability to secure its goals or impose its dominance in Lebanon, Syria, Iraq, and Afghanistan, have severely weakened the domestic political foundations of global military power to the point where the US public is opposed to sending large scale US ground troops into combat, leading to many executive promises which are subsequently broken

Nye's inventory of military resources, stockpile of up-to-date bombers, nuclear weapons, fighter planes, military bases, special forces operations, and its vast spy ("intelligence") apparatus—in other words the US's supreme military capacity—has not resulted in the establishment of a prosperous, stable, and submissive empire (the goal that Nye euphemistically dubs 'world supremacy'). US military engagements, in both high and low intensity wars, have resulted in costly defeats and retreats while adversaries advance into the vacuum. Superior material capacity has not translated into US dominance because nationalist, anti-imperialist consciousness and movements based on mass armed resistance have demonstrated superiority in countering foreign (US) invasions, occupations and satellite building.

Nye ignores a decisive military resource, which the US does not have and its adversaries have in abundance: nationalist consciousness. Here, Nye's notion of US supremacy in soft power has been terribly wrong-headed. According to Nye, the US superiority in the use and control of mass media, films, news and cultural organizations as well as educational institutions continues and has allowed the US to retain its global supremacy.

No doubt the US global propaganda apparatus and networks are formidable but they have not been successful, as a bulwark of US global supremacy. Once again Nye's inventory of soft power assets relies exclusively on quantitative, contemporary, material structures and ignores the enormous counter-influence of historical legacies, nationalist, cultural, religious, ethnic, class, race, and gender consciousness, which rejects US dominance in all of its forms. US soft power has neither conquered nor gained the allegiance of the peoples of Afghanistan, Iraq, Syria or Yemen. Nor has it convinced the billions of Russian, Chinese, Latin American or Islamic peoples to embrace American leadership.

No doubt soft power has worked to a limited extent, especially among sectors of the educated classes and the local political elite, converting them into imperial collaborators. No doubt elements of the educated elite have been co-opted by US funded 'non-governmental organizations' that engage in grass roots counter-insurgency as the counterpart to the drone attacks from above. But, once again, Nye relies on quantitative rather than qualitative measures of influence. Despite an army of NGOs and the budgeting of billions of dollars, US imperial conquests, coups, occupations, rigged elections, and puppet regimes are highly unpopular. As a result, US troops need to diminish their presence, and its overseas and visiting diplomats require a squadron of security officials and operate out of armed fortresses.

Professor Nye's treatment of what he calls soft power is reduced to an inventory of propaganda resources, developed and/or cultivated by the imperial state (the US) to induce submission to and acceptance of the global supremacy of the US. However vast the spending and however broad the scope of soft power he outlines, Nye fails to recognize the ineffectiveness of the US soft power apparatus in the face of systemic crimes against humanity, which have profoundly alienated and decisively turned world opinion and specific national publics against the US. Specifically, Washington's practice of torture (Abu Ghraib), kidnapping (rendition), and prolonged jailing without trial (Guantanamo); its global spy network monitoring hundreds of millions of citizens in the US and among allies, and its use of drones killing more non-combatant (innocent) citizens than armed adversaries, have severely weakened, if not undermined, the appeal of US soft powers. Nye is oblivious to the ways in which US projections of military power have led to the precipitous long-term decline of soft power, and the way in which that decline has resulted in the greater reliance on military power... in a vicious circle.

Nye ignores the changing composition of the strategic decision makers who decide where and when military power will be exercised. He blandly assumes that policy is directed by and for enhancing US global supremacy. But as Professors Mearsheimer and Walt (*The Israel Lobby*) and Petras (*The Power of Israel in the United States*) have demonstrated, powerful, organized lobbies, like AIPAC and Israel-First officials in the Executive branch, have taken military decisions leading the US to focus on the Middle East at the behest of Israel in order to enhance its power. These decisions have had an enormous cost in terms of loss of human and financial resources, and have contributed to the decline of US global supremacy. Nye fails to recognize how the ascendancy of his militarist colleagues in the Pentagon and the Zionists in the Congress and Executive have drastically changed the way in which hard (military) power is exercised—and how it has weakened the composition and use of soft power and provoked greater imbalances between economic and military power.

Nye's argument is further weakened by his incapacity to 'problematize' the changing content of military power: its shift from a tool of economic expansion, directed by US empire-builders, to becoming an end in itself, exploiting economic resources to enhance Israeli hegemony in the Middle East. This weakness is exacerbated by his failure to recognize the changing nature of economic power itself— the shift from manufacturing to finance capital and the negative consequences which result for the projection of US economic power and dominance.

Finally, Nye totally ignores the moral dimension of

the US drive for world dominance. At worst, he blithely assumes that destructive US wars are, by their nature—insofar as they are conducted by the exceptional American nation—virtuous. Nye's political commitment to the American Century and total belief in its benignancy blind him to the killing and displacement of millions of Iraqis, Syrians, Afghans, Somalis, Libyans, and now Ukrainians—among others. Nye's assumption of the beneficial effects of the US-NATO-EU expansion into the former Warsaw Pact countries, and especially Russia, ignores the vast impoverishment of 70% of the Ukrainian population, the outward flight of 20 million skilled professionals and workers, and the subsequent militarization of Eastern Europe and East Germany via its incorporation in NATO. According to Nye's moral calculus, any policy that enhances US global power is virtuous, no matter how it impacts the recipient population. These are not only Nye's views, they provide the ideological underpinning of the official soft power propaganda accompanying wars of mass destruction of the past, present, and near future.

Nye is not your typical garden variety Ivy League-ideologue-for-US-and-Israeli-dominance (and there are many in US academia). Nye has been an important theoretical architect and strategic planner responsible for US global wars and the accompanying crimes against humanity. His global fantasies of US ascendancy have led to the parlous state of the US domestic economy, multiple unwinnable wars overseas, and the eclipse of any strategic thinking about reversing the economic decline of the US in the world economy. Applying a cost-benefit analysis to Prof. Nye's policies—if he were employed as a CEO in the private sector, he would have long ago been fired and dispatched to a prestigious business school to teach 'ethics'. Since he is already tenured at Harvard and employed by the Pentagon he can continue to churn out his irresponsible manifestos of US global leadership and not be held to account for the disasters.

In Joseph Nye, we have our own American version of Colonel Blimp surveying his colonial projects: He has exchanged his pith helmet, short britches, and walking stick for a combat helmet and boots, and has limited his 'reviews' of the Empire to secure zones, surrounded by an entourage of combat-ready Leathernecks or mercenaries, circling helicopter warships and super-vetted local military toadies.

Historical Fallacies

Even at its zenith of global power during the 1940s, 50s and 60s, US military performance was the least effective component of world power as then exercised. Two major wars, Korea and Indo-China, speak against Nye's formula. The US military failed to defeat the North Korean and Chinese armies; Washington had to settle for a compromise. And the US was militarily defeated and forced to withdraw from Indo-China. Success in securing influence came afterwards, via economic investments and trade, accompanied by political and cultural influences.

Today, Nye's reliance on the superior military resources of the US to project the continuance of the American Century rests on very shaky historical foundations.

Nye's Military Metaphysics as Crackpot Realism

The US has declined as a world power because of its military pivot following Nye's military metaphysics and soft power psychobabble. In every practical situation where the US attempted to secure its dominance by relying on its superior military capacity against its competitors' reliance on economic and political resources, Washington has lost.

China has set in motion the Asian Infrastructure

Investment Bank (AIIB) with an initial offering of $50 billion dollars. The US is staunchly opposed to the AIIB because it clearly represents an alternative to the US-dominated International Monetary Fund (IMF). Despite Washington's pressure on them to reject membership, its allies, led by the UK and followed by all major powers (except Japan for now), have applied for membership. Even Israel has joined! Washington sought to convince leading emerging economies to accept US-centered economic integration, but instead, Brazil, Russia, India, China, and South Africa (the BRICS) founded the BRICS' bank.

The US engineered the overthrow of the elected government in the Ukraine, and set up a puppet regime to incorporate it as a NATO client and military platform on Russia's border. Instead, the Ukraine turned into an economic basket case, run by kleptocratic oligarchs, defended by openly neo-Nazi brigades, and incapable of defeating federal autonomist rebels in the industrialized east.

The US and the EU imposed economic sanctions on Russia and federal autonomist rebels of the Donbass in Eastern Ukraine. This has become another example of projecting political power to enlarge the scope of military operations at the cost of devastating losses in trade and investment between Moscow and the European Union, not to speak of the economic losses of the Ukraine, whose economy was dependent on trade with Russia.

The decline of US world power is, in part, a result of the dynamism and economic growth of emerging powers such as China and the relative decline of US market shares and inferior rates of growth.

Nye, in one of his more egregiously foolish efforts to puff up US economic superiority and to downgrade China's economic rise, argues that China's growth rate is 'likely to slow in the future'. Dear Joe... don't you know that a

Chinese 'slowdown' from double digit growth to seven percent is still triple the rate of growth of the US today and for the foreseeable future?

Moreover China's economy, balanced between production and finance, is less crisis-prone than the lopsided growth of the US economy reliant on and milked by the corrupt US financial sector. Nye's economic calculus ignores the qualitative, as well as quantitative, dimensions of economic power.

Conclusion

The dubious intellectual value of Joseph Nye's writings would not merit serious consideration except for the fact that they have a deep and abiding influence on US foreign policy. Nye is an ardent advocate of empire building, and his arguments and prescriptions carry weight in the White House and Pentagon. His normative bias and his love of empire building blind him to objective realities. The fact that he is a failed policy advisor, who refuses to acknowledge the defeats, decline, and destruction resulting from his world view, has not lessened the dangerous nature of his current views.

Nye's attempt to justify his vision of continuing US world supremacy has led him to blame his critics. In his latest book, he rants that predictions of US decline are 'dangerous' because they could encourage countries such as China to pursue more aggressive policies. In other words, having failed, through logic and facts, to sustain his assertions against his better-informed critics, Nye questions their loyalty—evoking a McCarthyite specter of intellectuals critical of US global power stabbing the country in the back.

Nye tries to deflect attention from the fragile material

foundations of US power to disembodied perceptions. According to Nye, it's all about perceptions (or illusions!): if the world leaders and public believe that the American century is set to continue for many decades, that conviction will, in itself, help to sustain America's superiority! Nye's political analysis is unlikely to convince any serious analyst beyond the halls of the Pentagon and Harvard University's John F Kennedy School.

What matters is that the US, while it is a declining world power, is still militarily powerful, dangerous and destructive, even as its empire building is weakening and its forces are in retreat. As Mahatma Gandhi once stated about the declining British Empire, 'It's the aging tiger that becomes the man eater'.

As an alternative, we can follow two lines of inquiry: One is to question the entire imperial enterprise and to focus on our return to republican values and domestic social and democratic reconstruction. That is a necessary, but prolonged struggle, under present circumstances. In the meantime, we can pursue policies that emphasize the importance of shifting from destructive military expansionism toward constructive economic engagements, flexible cooperation with emerging competitors, and diplomatic agreements with adversaries. Contrary to Nye's assertions, militarism and economic expansion are not compatible. Wars destroy markets and occupations provoke resistance, which frighten investors. Soft power and NGO's that rely on manipulation, lies, and demonization of critics gain few adherents and multiple adversaries.

The US should increase its ties and co-operation with BRICS and China's AIIB. It should reach out to sign trade deals with Iran, and cease its support for actions against Syria and Lebanon. It should cut off aid to Israel, because of it bellicose posture toward the Arab East and its brutal colonization of Palestine. Washington should end its support of violent coups and engage with Venezuela. It should lift sanctions against Russia and East Ukraine and propose joint economic ventures. By ending colonial wars, we can increase economic growth and open markets. We should pursue economic accommodation not military occupation. The former leads to prosperity, the latter to destruction.

Endnotes

1   *Financial Times*, 3/26/15, p. 7.

| Chapter Thirteen |

A CRITIQUE OF THE CFR'S "REVISING US GRAND STRATEGY TOWARD CHINA"

"We will have a very strong (military) presence, very strong continued posture throughout the region to back our commitments to our allies, to protect and work with our partners and to continue ensuring peace and stability in the region, as well as back our diplomacy vis-à-vis China on the South China Sea".[1]
David Shear, Assistant Secretary of Defence for Asian and Pacific Security Affairs

Indian President Modi *"seals $22 billion of deals on China visit ... China had already promised $20 billion of infrastructure investment during [Chinese President] Xi's visit to India last year"*.
Financial Times[2]

Introduction

The highly influential Council on Foreign Relations recently published a Special Report entitled "Revising US

Grand Strategy toward China",[3] co-authored by two of its Senior Fellows, Robert Blackwill and Ashley Tellis, which proposes a re-orientation of US policy toward China. The Report projects a policy for buttressing 'US primacy in Asia' and countering what they describe as "the dangers that China's geo-economic and military power pose to US national interests in Asia and globally". The Report concludes by listing seven recommendations that Washington should follow to re-assert regional primacy.

We begin by discussing the basic fallacies underpinning the Report, including its outdated and dangerous presumptions about US power and presence in Asia today, and the authors' incoherent, contradictory, and unrealistic prescriptions.

Mistaken Assumptions about Past and Present US Policies to China

Blackwill and Tellis (B&T) start out with the preposterous claim that contemporary US policy toward China has been driven by its positive "effort to 'integrate' China into the liberal international order". This is a gross misrepresentation of Washington's past and current efforts to subvert the Chinese Communist government and to undermine its state-directed transition to capitalism.

Ever since the end of the Second World War, and especially since the Chinese Civil War (1945-49), which brought the Chinese Communist Party to power, the US has poured billions of dollars in military aid to the retreating Nationalist regime and to finance the bloody Korean War (1950-53) with the open goal of overthrowing the Chinese communist government. When US forces briefly reached the Chinese-Korean border, provoking a Chinese response, Washington threatened to unleash nuclear weapons on the

Chinese. For the next two decades, the US maintained a naval and air embargo against the world's most populous state, an insane policy which was only reversed by President Nixon's re-establishment of diplomatic and commercial relations in 1973.

When the veteran Chinese leader, Deng Xiaoping, embarked on a state-managed transition to capitalism, Washington adopted a two-track policy of encouraging China's rulers to 'open their markets' to US multi-national corporations, while financing and backing Chinese pro-US liberal activists seeking to overthrow the Communist government (the so-called Tiananmen Square Uprising) as well as the secessionist Tibetan and Uyghur insurgencies in western China.

Far from trying "to integrate China into the liberal international order", Washington attempted to replicate the decade-long chaotic and destructive "transition to capitalism" which took place with the dissolution of the USSR under Mikhail Gorbachev. During the disastrous US-backed regime of Russian President Boris Yeltsin—the 'lost decade' (1990-1999)—living standards for the average citizen plunged 70% and Russia was transformed from an advanced superpower to a ravaged vassal state. Beijing's rulers took careful stock of the grotesque pillage of the former USSR and rejected US plans to replicate their 'Russian success' and integrate China as a vassal state within the international capitalist system.

Washington's sanctions and boycott policy, following the defeat of its Tiananmen Square proxies, was of no avail: Washington failed to stop the massive influx of US multinational corporations into China. Its punitive measures had no impact on China's political stability and unprecedented economic growth.

Washington's policy supporting China's entry into the World Trade Organization was intended to encourage

China to open up to US investors, but US policymakers did not understand how the Chinese state's carefully calibrated mix of dependence on foreign capitalist investment and technology with their adoption, assimilation, and autonomous expansion of endogenous Chinese expertise would create a such a massive independent economic superpower.

Washington's 'penetration and conquest strategy', dubbed by B &T as its 'integration into the international order,' ultimately failed, despite frequent attempts to undermine the Chinese state regulations and controls on foreign capital. The US effort to subordinate ("integrate") China into its burgeoning Asian empire was unsuccessful. During this period, China expanded into world markets, harnessing Western capital to its national goals. It borrowed and improved on US technology to develop a high growth model, exceeding the US growth rate by six-fold—12% versus 2%.

For over two decades, China grew exponentially, accumulating hundreds of billions of dollars in foreign reserves, while the US economy ran up monstrous trade deficits with Beijing. The US had embarked on a series of prolonged wars while converting its economy from productive to finance capitalism and needed to borrow vast sums from China in the form of sales of Treasury notes or face a major domestic financial crisis.

In essence (and not noted by B&T), China 'integrated' into the international economic order as a productive, creditor state, at the same time the US was reduced to financial–debtor status and lost its global economic primacy while pursuing its unpopular wars in the Middle East.

It was not the failure of liberal US market policies that propelled China forward to primacy in Asia, as B&T argue in their essay, but Washington's multi-trillion-dollar wars in South Asia, the Middle East, and North Africa, and its wholesale conversion to Wall Street speculation, which caused the US to lose its primacy in Asia. While US 'market liberalism' did give China access to markets, permitted corporate production and export of its products, B&T's claim that it helped China to emerge as the economic superpower in Asia is a flimsy pretext for ignoring real causes and now promoting an even greater level of US militarism in the region. Unfortunately, their muddle-headed diagnoses and militarist proposals strongly influence the Obama Administrations policy decisions!

Blackwill and Tellis's unwillingness to recognize China's peaceful rise to economic supremacy in Asia leads them to rely on a purely ideological construct to bolster their militaristic argument for intensifying "the US naval and air presence in the South and East China Seas and accelerating the US ballistic-missile defense [sic] posture" in the Pacific. B&T's a priori ideological presumptions lead them to declare that "China is a danger to US Asian interests", ignoring elementary Chinese vital national interests in having open and secure access to vital waterways leading to their Asian markets and global sources of raw materials. At no point does B&T identify a single move implemented by China, which has threatened the open seaways. Nor do they identify a single overt or covert threat by China toward the US.

While B&T speculate about China's military threats, they suffer a severe case of amnesia with regard to overt US attacks, invasions, and occupations of China's Asian neighbors. Over a dozen such military assaults have been launched by Washington in the region, which B&T conveniently omit. The US has recently dispatched B-1 bombers and surveillance planes to Australia and threatens to attack China's base and port construction on its off-shore shoals and island territories.[1] Equally ominous, US officials arrested a visiting Chinese academic attending a conference, claiming he was part of a plot to steal 'dual purpose' high tech secrets.

Contradictions and Incoherence in B&T's Policy Recommendations

B&T policy recommendations for securing US primacy in Asia are contradictory and incoherent. While they recommend that the US "revitalize the economy" and promote "robust growth" as a first priority, they then demand a "substantial increase" in the enormous US military budget. Their advocacy of limits on the sale of civilian technology (so-called "dual" use) reiterates a discussion of long standing, while their proposal to exclude China from US-sponsored Asian trade networks like the Trans-Pacific Partnership (TPP) has already occurred.

Most experts openly acknowledge that the huge US ten-trillion-dollar military spending over the past two decades has destroyed any possibility for robust growth of the US economy. B&T's recommendations for even more military spending can only make matters worse by diverting public and private capital away from economic growth. This is what undermines the United States strategic future in Asia!

B&T advise Washington "to expand Asian trade networks" ... by excluding China, the largest investment site and market for the leading '500' US multi-national corporations! In fact, when Obama, in line with B&T recommendations, loudly refused to participate in the Chinese-sponsored 'Asian Infrastructure Investment Bank, all of the US major Asian 'partners', except Japan (which hosts 130 US bases), ignored Washington and joined the AIIB! China is unquestionably the leading economic partner for all Asian countries and none of the bellicose rhetoric that

B&T spout is going to erode those essential realities, nor will whatever economic growth the US could manage.

In fact B&T's reiteration of long-discussed proposals to eliminate ongoing trade with China of so-called dual purpose technological exports will further isolate the US from its much-ballyhooed Asian partners, who are especially eager to add value to their exports. In sum, B&T's recommendations to US policy makers will guarantee an anemic, not a robust, growth, as they clearly are guided by a strictly military logic, contrary to advancing US trade networks.

B&T (and the Obama regime) propose "to reinforce" what they call the Indo-Pacific partnership via a "build-up (of) the power-political capabilities of its friends and allies on China's periphery", such as having Vietnam or the Philippines take China to the World Court concerning claims in the South China Sea. However, they avoided considering the position of the largest and most significant of those countries—India—and its drive for economic development and long-term, large-scale investment and trade agreements. The meager trade and development results following from Obama's recent visit to India demonstrate just how shallow the administration's policy towards the subcontinent really is.

The Indo-Chinese economic and development partnership far surpasses in size and scope any of the vacuous proposals put forth by B&T to the Obama Administration. In mid-May 2015, Indian President Modi signed a $22 billion business deal with China on top of the massive $20-billion Chinese infrastructure investment agreement in 2014. These $42 billion of Chinese investment and trade deals with India have pulled the rug out from under any Obama regime plans to enlist India into its anti-China campaign and military provocations. The reality of Indian-Chinese economic deals shows just how absurd B& T policy recommendations are.

President Modi put the nail in the coffin of B&T's "Revising US Grand Strategy toward China" in his last speech while in China following his most successful visit. "I strongly believe that this century belongs to Asia," he stated. Lest it be thought by any other Kissinger protégé (Blackwill is a Henry Kissinger Senior Fellow) that the deepening Indo-China relation is a mere passing phenomenon, their agreements involve the most advanced sectors of their economies, including telecommunication and energy, as well as the development of a solar photovoltaic industrial park.

As for B&T's proposal to block dual use technology transfers to China, the Indian government has openly rejected that line of unreason by calling on countries to accelerate technology transfers.

B&T and the entire crowd of armchair war-mongers at the Council on Foreign Relations (CFR) have misread the most basic economic developments of our time. US economic growth is becoming increasingly dependent on large-scale, long-term foreign capital inflows from 'emerging economies'—especially China! Developing Asian nations accounted for $440 billion in outward investment, making them the largest source of foreign direct investment, greater than North America or Europe. China's $266 billion dollars accounted for most outgoing FDI from Asia.

China's importance as a source of investment can only expand, especially through its newly-founded Asian Infrastructure Investment Bank (AIIB) and its plans to promote the multi-billion Silk Road linking Beijing through Central Asia to European markets. China's financial role is going to be crucial in the new BRICS (Brazil, Russia, India, China and South Africa) bank, developed to counter the IMF.

Nothing that the Obama regime and its advisers from the Council on Foreign Relations have proposed can possibly balance the rise of China, because their policies include the boycott of large-scale, long-term Chinese economic initiatives which Washington's allies are eager to join. Virtually all have rushed to sign up with the AIIB leaving a sour-faced Obama Administration totally isolated. The Council on Foreign Relations' proposal for Obama to form anti-Chinese networks with its allies is pointless when such hostile networks are clearly not going to undermine their most lucrative economic deals with China.

After running through a laundry list of hostile policies toward China based on a strategy of escalating military encirclement, B&T conclude their essay with a bizarre call for Washington to "energize high level diplomacy with Beijing" and do "everything it can to avoid a confrontation with China". Of course, related to the actuality of the situation, this is contradictory. But perhaps this suggestion of energizing high-level diplomacy has more to do with a campaign to publicly paint the US as doing everything it can to avoid confrontation, hoping/trusting that the noise of same would overcome the facts on the ground in public perception, keeping US "white-knight" image.

Policies designed to surround China with US military installations and naval vessels, threaten China's vital maritime routes. Measures to restrict the sale of dual use (civilian) technology and efforts to build hostile regional networks and military partnerships are hardly conducive to energizing high level diplomacy with Beijing, and have been unsuccessfully proposed for decades. B&T's proposals and Obama's policies are designed to confront, provoke, and undermine China. That is one very obvious reason why China pursues such favorable economic agreements with its neighbors.

B&T policy proposals are doomed to fail because the US has not and cannot match China's robust economic growth. Washington cannot compete with Beijing's open and flexible large-scale economic agreements with all Asian countries (even Japan, the US vassal, Japan, now exports more to China than to the US).

Most Asian powers have rejected the ideological message peddled by the Obama Administration that China is a danger. They see China as a partner, a source of capital and easy financing for vital projects without the onerous conditions that the US-controlled IMF imposes. They are not interested in big, wasteful spending on costly weapons systems pushed by US war industries, which have no productive value.

An Alternative "Grand Strategy toward China"

If one were to propose a realistic and reasonable US Grand Strategy toward China one would have to start by shedding all the false assumptions and bellicose proposals that have been put forth by the CFR and the authors of the Report under review. These include:

1. The US should give up its self-appointed role as global policeman, reallocate its bloated Pentagon budget to finance vital domestic economic development, while rebalancing the US economy away from Wall Street speculation in the FIRE (finance, insurance real estate) sector, towards producing goods, providing quality services, and financing long-overdue infrastructure development projects.

2. Washington should expand and promote long-term, large-scale exports of its advanced technology to compensate for the loss of low value exports.

3. Washington should join with China in its new infrastructure bank, securing contracts via aid packages. Washington would have to look at China's export of

capital as an opportunity to improve the US's deteriorating infrastructure.

4. Washington should replace its military bases surrounding China with industrial parks, commercial ports and regional 'Silicon Valleys' and promote co-operative ventures that allow the US to ride the wave of Chinese dynamism. It would have to increase and expand its cyber-technical ties with China via joint ventures. Since the US cannot (and should not) curtail or compete with China's growth it should join them and share it.

5. The US should not attempt to block China's growth and expansion; it should assist and share in its ascendancy, especially in the face of great global climate and energy challenges. Washington is much more likely to strengthen its Asian-Pacific partnership and succeed in its diplomacy if it replaced its military posturing with robust economic growth.

Endnotes

1   Michelle Florcruz, "US Defense Official 'Misspoke' On China B-1 Bomber And Surveillance Plan In Australia," " http://www.ibtimes.com/us-defense-official-misspoke-china-b-1-bomber-surveillance-plan-australia-1924347>
2   *Financial Times*, 5/18/16, p. 4
3   Robert Blakwill and Ashley Tellis, "Revising US Grand Strategy Towards China," Council on Foreign Relations Press: NY 2015,

| Chapter Fourteen |

WESTERN MAINSTREAM MEDIA EXTREMISM: THE LIES OF OUR TIMES

Introduction

With the collapse of the Communist countries in the 1990s and their conversion to capitalism, followed by the advent of neoliberal regimes throughout most of Latin America, Asia, Europe and North America, the imperial regimes in the US and EU established a new political spectrum, in which the standards of acceptability narrowed and the definition of adversaries expanded. Over the past quarter century, the US and EU turned their focus from systemic adversaries (anti-capitalist and anti-imperial states and movements) to attacking capitalist regimes, which (1) had adopted nationalist, re-distributive and Keynesian policies; (2) had opposed military interventions, coups and bases; (3) had aligned with non-Western capitalist powers; (4) had opposed Zionist colonization of Palestine and Gulf State-financed Islamist terrorists; (5) or had refused to follow the financial agendas dictated by Wall Street and the City of London investment houses, speculators and vulture funds.

The Western imperial regimes (by which we mean the US, Canada and the EU) have exercised their political, military, economic, and propaganda powers to (1) eliminate or limit the variety of capitalist options; (2) control the kinds of market-state relations; and (3) secure compliance through punitive military invasions, occupations and economic sanctions against targeted adversaries.

The Media Troika: The Financial Press and Political Warfare

The major financial newspapers of record in the United States played a key role in disseminating the post-communist political line regarding what are acceptable capitalist policies: The *Wall Street Journal,* (WSJ), *The New York Times* (NYT), and the *Financial Times* (FT)—the 'Troika'—have systematically engaged in political warfare, acting as virtual propaganda arms of the US and EU imperialist governments in their attempts to maintain and/or impose vassal state status on countries and economies, which are or to be regulated according to the needs of Western financial institutions.

The propaganda Troika not only reflects the interests and policies of the ruling elites, but their editors, journalists and commentators also shape policies through their reportage, analyses and editorials.

The Troika's methods of political operation and the substance of their policies preclude any kind of balanced reportage.

Day in and day out, the Troika fabricates crises for adversaries and illusory promises of recovery for vassals, and distorts and/or omits favorable information regarding adversaries, dismissing targeted regimes as 'authoritarian' and 'corrupt'. In contrast, obedient and submissive rulers are described as 'pragmatic' and 'realist'. The Troika attributes 'military threats' and 'aggressive behavior' to adversaries engaged in defensive policies, while labeling vassal state invasions or aggression as justified, retaliatory or defensive.

A close reading of the reportage by the stable of Troika scribes over the past two years reveals the repeated use of vitriolic and highly charged terms in describing adversarial leaders. This prepares the reader for the one-sided, negative assessment of past, present, and future policies adopted by the targeted regime.

Once the imperial states and the Troika decide on targeting a government and its leaders, all the subsequent 'news' is designed to present the motives of these leaders as perfidious and the economic and social impact of their policies as catastrophic.

And whenever the Troika's analyses or predictions or prognostications turned out to be blatantly wrong—there are never corrections (though there was the NYT's apology for its misleading coverage that led to the 2003 invasion of Iraq, an apology which did not alter its misrepresentations then going forward). Brazen lies are glossed over with nary a ripple in their smooth fabric of propaganda.

Once a government is designated as enemy (thereby ripe for regime change), the Troika recycles the same hostile messages almost daily. The readers, upon viewing Troika headlines, already know at least three quarters of the content of the article. A small portion of a report may refer tangentially to some particular event or policy decision for which the diatribe has been launched.

Working hand-in-hand with Western imperial regimes, the Troika targets the same regimes as they do, using the exact same terms dished out by imperial policy spokesmen and women.

In this chapter, we will discuss the main regimes

and policies targeted by the Troika and its Western imperial state partners. We will then proceed to evaluate Troika facts, interpretations, and their track record from the beginning of the onslaught to the present. We will conclude by examining the conversion of the mainstream 'serious' financial press into a triumvirate of tub-thumping warmongers.

Trumpeting Targeted Regimes' Sins and Denying Their Successes

The Troika's propaganda war not only converges with the imperial states' destabilization policies (regime change) but also is aimed at specific policies and agreements among supposed allies, partners, and even vassal states.

The intensity of vitriol and the frequency of hostile articles vary according to the level of conflict between the imperial regime and its target for regime change. The greater the conflict the more violent the language.

We find intense Troika hostility, in the form of frequent, hysterical attacks, directed against Russia, China, Iran, Venezuela, Argentina, and Palestine. Even any suspected deviations by vassals, like Chile or pre-coup Brazil, in the form of popular domestic social legislations, are subjected to stern scolding and warnings of dire consequences.

The Troika Maligns Russia

In the case of Russia, the Troika routinely denounces President Vladimir Putin as an authoritarian ruler who has undermined Russian democracy. They claim Russia's economy is in crisis and facing imminent collapse. They vilify Russia's military assistance to the Syrian government of Bashar al-Assad. They question the viability of Russia's military treaties and economic agreements with China.

In sum, the Troika portrays Russia as a once peaceful, democratic law-abiding country (during the kleptocratic years of Boris Yeltsin in the 1990s), which has been taken over by former secret KGB officials who have embarked on reckless overseas military adventures, while repressing their own ethnic Muslim populations (in Chechnya and Dagestan) and which is being run into the ground because of mismanagement and (deserved) Western economic sanctions. They never bother to explain why the 'authoritarian' Putin maintains a consistently high citizen approval despite the Troika's litany of evils...

Troika-Backed Ukrainian Puppet Secures 1% Approval

In December 2013, US Assistant Secretary of State for European and Eurasian Affairs Victoria Nuland, the foul mouthed diplomat, puppet dominatrix and austerity zealot, bragged that Washington had poured $5 billion dollars into Ukraine in order to pursue regime change and install a puppet regime headed by President Petro Poroshenko and ('Our man, Yats') Arseniy Yatsenyuk as Prime Minister. Obedient to his Western sponsors and the Troika, Yatsenyuk proceeded to sign off on an IMF bailout and austerity program, slashing salaries and pensions of Ukrainian citizens by half, reducing GNP by 25%, ending fuel and food subsidies, and tripling unemployment. These policies brought windfall profits for Ukraine's billionaire crony capitalists and intensified corruption. The Troika labelled the Nuland putsch a 'democratic revolution', applauding Yastenyuk for vigorously applying the IMF-dictated program, and predicted a prosperous future...

As discontent spread and anger mounted among Ukrainian citizens, Yatsenyuk continued to feed his own ego by reading the Troika's puff-piece editorials lauding his courage for staying the course of austerity and ignoring his compatriots' opinion polls, up until the October 25, 2015 elections.

As the elections neared, opinion polls revealed that 99% of the electorate (which excluded millions of restive citizens of the Donbass region) completely rejected Arseniy (now known as 'Nuland's arsehole') Yatsenyuk. Faced with the universal rejection of his starvation policies and crony capitalism, he withdrew his party (the Popular [sic] Front) from the election, but not from the 'democratic' government...

For two years the Troika had praised the Kiev junta, fabricating reports about Kiev's positive economic reforms ... which had benefited the 1% corrupt oligarchs while impoverishing the masses. The Western propaganda mills systematically distorted popular reaction among the Ukrainian citizens, citing imaginary 'anonymous experts' and phantom 'men in the street' in praise of the debacle. Never had the Troika engaged in such blatantly deceptive journalism as its account of the two years of pillage and mass immiseration under Prime Minister Yatsenyuk. And when 'Yats' was faced with total repudiation, he blithely dismissed Ukrainian public opinion, claiming he was "not concerned by temporary [sic] political party ratings". His indifference when faced with an electoral repudiation of 99% is rooted in a delusion that he will remain Prime Minister because he is widely praised by the EU, the US, the IMF ... and the media Troika.

The Troika and China: Here Comes the Crash ... ?

In its journalistic pivot to Asia, the Troika deprecates China's high-growth economy by questioning its data and by repeatedly predicting an impending crisis, breakdown and mass disaffection.

The Troika describes China's defense policy as a

military threat to its neighbors, and labels its overseas trade and investment policies as neo-colonial exploitation.

China's national campaign against corruption and its prosecution of corrupt officials is dismissed by the Troika as a political purge by a power-hungry president.

The Troika attributes Chinese advances in science and technology as mere cyber-theft of Western innovations.

The movement of Chinese workers (internal migration) to areas with better paying jobs and investments is called colonization.

The Chinese government's response to terrorism and armed separatists from Tibet and the Western Uighur regions is denounced as Beijing's systematic violation of the human rights of minorities.

The Troika Castigates Capitalist Argentina (for a Decade of Growth)

Argentina has been on the Troika's radar for a decade, despite the fact that its center-left government had rescued capitalism from a total collapse (the crisis of 1998-2002), restoring the growth of profits. Multinationals, like Monsanto and Chevron, enjoy huge returns on their investments in Argentina.

The Troika denounced that government for running up budget deficits while ignoring the impact of a Manhattan court judgement to award a group of Wall Street vulture fund speculators interest payments of one-thousand percent on old pre-crisis debt.

The Troika claimed the regime engaged in populist excesses, which prevent large-scale inflows of investment capital.

The Troika described the recent slowdown in the economy as a deep crisis, which requires deep structural changes (namely the elimination of social funding for pensioners, low income wage earners and school children).

The Troika painted a catastrophic picture of Argentina: a decaying economy run by a demagogic political leadership engaged in falsifying data to mask an imminent collapse...

The Troika's 'Hate Venezuela' Campaign

The Troika's journalists and editorial writers portray Venezuela as an unmitigated disaster: a stagnant and collapsing economy, ruined by an authoritarian populist regime repressing peaceful opposition dissenters.

According to the Troika, Venezuela is incapable of providing basic goods to consumers. Instead it resorts to draconian confiscation of goods from honest businesses unjustly accused of hoarding and profiteering. The daily reality of manufactured 'shortages' is consistently ignored.

When the Venezuelan government attempts to stop violent cross border raids by Colombian paramilitary gangs and smugglers it is denounced as arbitrarily repressing Colombian immigrants.

When Caracas arrests opposition leaders for their well-documented involvement in violent street demonstrations, for promoting the sabotage of power plants and clinics, and for planning coups, they are portrayed as violating the human rights of legitimate dissidents.

The Troika never mentions the tens of millions of US dollars provided by Washington to opposition NGOs to pursue its destabilization campaign against Venezuela. It labels US-funded opposition NGO's as "independent civil society organizations" (just as it labeled Nuland's $5 billion-supported NGOs in Ukraine before the putsch).

For almost two decades, the Troika has praised Venezuelan opposition groups as formidable critics of the

Chavez-Maduro government, but has never explained to their readers why such 'formidable' groups have been soundly defeated in 14 of the 15 elections.

The Troika and Palestine: In Defense of Israeli Terror

In its Middle East coverage, the Troika consistently depicts the Palestinians as violent terrorists and aggressors while describing Israelis as their victims. According to the Troika, the Israeli army is engaged in justifiable 'reprisals' when they bomb and slaughter Palestinian civilians trapped in Gaza. The endless dispossession of Palestinians of their homes, farms, and rights, and the violent settler occupation by Israeli Jewish colonists is presented as the just settlement of Jews escaping persecution.

No mention or little importance is given to Israeli-Jewish desecration of Islamic and Christian religious sites or Israeli systematic terror and mass jailing of peaceful protesters. Palestinian resistance is described as incendiary, irrational violence.

The Troika journalists produce articles which are virtually indistinguishable from the press handouts of the Zionist Power Configuration in the US. The Troika even chastises their partner US-EU regimes for any bland criticism or expression of shock at Israel's most egregious crimes.

The Troika echoes Israeli and Zionist attacks on international tribunals charging Israeli officials with crimes against humanity. The Troika claims they lack 'balance' though the casualty figures of the conflict themselves are extraordinarily 'unbalanced.'

The Troika and Syria: Armchair Generals

The Troika has demonized the Syrian government

of Bashar al-Assad while backing jihadi terrorists dubbed rebels or 'moderates.' It has long argued for greater direct military intervention by NATO armies to overthrow the government in Damascus.

The Troika, masquerading as independent 'financial press,' publishes scores of articles by dozens of armchair generals who concoct military strategies against Damascus while ignoring their heavy economic costs, the social catastrophe of four million internal and external Syrian war refugees, and the grave consequences of the splitting up a once-unified secular nation-state.

The Troika and Wayward Neoliberals

The Troika even chastises states and governments which have adopted 'free market policies' but maintained or introduced moderate social palliatives to assuage their negative impact on citizens. For example, the Chilean regime of Michelle Bachelet fell victim to Troika criticism for promoting a mild increase in corporate taxes and implementing trade union legislation allowing for greater workers' rights. According to the Troika, these mild reforms have led to economic stagnation, a decline in investment and greater social polarization.

The Troika's Primary Denigration Techniques: Distortion, Fabrication, and Falsification

The Troika's journalism and editorializing on Russia has totally distorted its recent political and economic history. Like all confidence men, Troika journalists and editors mix a few threads of facts with patent falsehoods, magnifying defects and minimizing achievements, ignoring positive long-term trends and emphasizing episodic negatives.

The Troika's accounts of Russia's recent military and diplomatic assistance to the Syrian government's struggle against Islamist terrorists ignore its achievement in reversing IS advances—which purportedly the West is seeking.

The Troika paints a specter of 'Great Russian geopolitical expansion' and ignores the long-standing political partnerships and alliances between Russia and major countries in the region, Iraq, Iran, Lebanon, Syria and Jordan.

With matters economic, the Troika describes the 'catastrophic' impact of US-EU sanctions against Russia over Ukraine, while ignoring the positive long-term results for Russia's economy—greater self-reliance and investment in manufacturing and agriculture as a stimulus to local producers, and the emergence of alternative overseas suppliers and markets, especially China and Iran.

The Troika highlights Russia's two-year recession while ignoring a decade and a half of substantial growth after the catastrophic Yeltsin years.

The Troika falsifies past and present political developments. They discreetly praise the Russia ruled by Western-backed, violent gangster-oligarchs during the pillage years of the 1990s as a democracy while denouncing the the Putin Presidency as authoritarian, despite wide acknowledgement of his great popularity.

The Troika resorts to similar propaganda ploys with China. Any slowdown from China's three decades of double digit growth gets spun as an imminent collapse, ignoring the fact that the US-European business community can only dream of China's still robust growth rate of 7%.

The allegations of Chinese cyber theft of Western science and technology ignore the obvious fact that China's enormous public investment in basic and applied science and technology in dozens of centers of excellence has produced stunning achievements and levels of scholarship. A review of the international scientific literature and journals paints an entirely different picture of Chinese advances from that described by the Troika.

Chinese economic growth through seaborne exports requires major investment and commitment to its maritime routes and security. To counter Chinese growth and assert US supremacy, Washington has signed new, provocative military pacts with Japan, Australia, and the Philippines, and escalated the intrusion of its planes and ships into Chinese waters and airspace. The Troika labels China's defense of its waterways as an aggressive military threat to its regional neighbors, while US military investments in bases throughout Asia and constant intelligence gathering exceed Beijing's fivefold. US warships brazenly violate China's 12 mile maritime boundary.

Troika scribes completely ignore the recent history of US and Japanese empires invading Asian countries, establishing colonies, and killing millions of people. In contrast to the enormous US strategic ring of military bases and communications outposts throughout the Asia-Pacific region, China has only one foreign base—in Djibouti, if 2016 negotiations are successfully concluded—a fact one will never learn from the Troika.

The Troika's campaign against Argentina, permeating its pages, minimizes the role of a short-term contemporary slow-down in international demand for commodities and attributes Argentina's problems to its welfare programs, capital controls and state regulation. The Troika fails to acknowledge the past decade of growth, prosperity and rising living standards among the people in Argentina.

The source of Argentine stagnation is not because of a lack of free market policies but due to the Fernandez regime's forced accommodation and promotion of the interests of international bankers—virtually all foreign debt holders (except one notorious foreign vulture!) and extractive capitalists (agribusiness, Monsanto, Barrack Gold etc.).

The Troika ignores the 1990s 'decade of infamy' during which Argentina served as a bargain bazaar for the privatization of lucrative public enterprises and eventually collapsed in the 2001 crash with major bank closings, one hundred thousand bankruptcies and five million unemployed (30% of the labor force)—a thoroughly pillaged economy. Instead the Troika fabricates an ideal world of past free market prosperity in order to condemn contemporary Argentine, ignoring the real historical record of a liberal debacle and Keynesian recovery.

Venezuela is currently in a severe crisis, as the Troika scribes remind us in their shrill reports—blaming it entirely on 'populist' (i.e. public) spending on social welfare and 'nationalist' policies.

The Troika ignores the well-documented sabotage by the importers and distributers in the private business community, hoarding, excess profiteering, and currency speculation and flight. These problems are exacerbated by the sharp decline of oil revenues resulting from international market forces, and not merely government mismanagement.

The Troika tells their readers that the Chavez and Maduro governments are authoritarian, ignoring the dozen and a half free and competitive elections since Chavez' ascent to power. Moreover, the Troika has remained rather quiet over their verbally violent editorial support for the opposition business-led and US embassy-backed military coup in 2002 and an aborted coup again in 2014.

Conclusion

The Troika—the *Wall Street Journal, The New York*

Times and the *Financial Times*—have repeatedly made false prognoses regarding the economic performances of governments targeted for regime change. Their economic predictions were repeatedly wrong and their readers among the investor public would have lost their shirts if they had taken their cues from the Troika's editorial pages and bet 'short' against China and the rest.

Their perverse denunciations of Russian and Chinese military defense activities are sharpening world tensions. Their support for ethnic separatists in the Russian Caucuses and western China has encouraged acts of terrorism leading to the deaths of hundreds of Chinese workers murdered by Uighur and Tibetan terrorists, hundreds of Russians at hands of Chechen terrorists,[1] and thousands of Russian-speakers in Ukraine's Donbass region.

The Troika cannot be relied on for reliable information, especially regarding the economic, political, and foreign policies of US and EU adversaries (those targeted for regime change).

At most their polemical screeds give the discerning reader an insight into the propaganda line promoted by the Western powers, and the techniques by which they do so.

Significantly, in recent times, the Troika has become even more strident and militaristic than the ruling elites. The Troika's armchair generals mocked Obama for not sending ground troops into Syria; chastised the US and EU for signing the nuclear agreements with Iran; and embraced Israel's systematic murder of Palestinians.

Unreliable and more given to strident invective than reporting the facts in a balanced way, the Troika has lost credibility for intelligent, serious readers who strain to 'read between the lines' when they write that a government is 'unpopular' during elections. More likely than not, the incumbents sweep the elections and retain popular majorities as was the case in Russia, Argentina, and Venezuela until 2015.

If and when the Troika succeeds in promoting more wars, as it has been doing in Iraq, Libya, Syria, Yemen and Somalia, each and every militaristic adventure will lead to economic and social disasters spawning millions more refugees.

When imperial governments, like England, adopt conciliatory policies toward China, eschewing zero sum confrontations, in favor of win-win cooperation, the Troika's armchair generals are sure to mock and accuse the conservative government of 'kowtowing' to authoritarians—dismissing the $30 billion dollar investment deals.

The Troika has gone far beyond its earlier role of presenting the line of imperial regimes. They now march to the military drum of real and imagined nuclear warriors and terrorists. Welcome to the "free press" and the lies of our times!

Endnotes

1 On the other hand, the Russians destroyed the Chechen city of Grozny (their name—named by the inhabitants Jalalabad…), and the apartment terrorism blamed on Chechens was likely not done by them. Even the Moscow theatre hostage deaths resulted mostly from the rescue attempts which gave rise to them, reminiscent of the Munich athlete deaths.

PART THREE

LEFTISTS AND ISLAMISTS

| Chapter Fifteen |

THE LEFT: BUSINESS ACCOMMODATION AND SOCIAL DEBACLE

Prologue

In 2004 I wrote *Brazil and Lula: Year Zero*[1] in which I presented my analysis of the Lula-Workers' Party (PT) regime in Brazil undergoing a grand transformation with the first stage represented by the PT's incorporation into a government apparatus led by of bankers and exporters (the agro-mineral elite). Two years earlier, my colleague, Henry Veltmeyer, and I had published *Cardoso's Brazil: A Land for Sale*[2] where we described how President Cardoso had sold off the major public resources, banks, petroleum, and iron resources to foreign capital for rock-bottom prices. The 2002 election of President Lula da Silva of the Workers' Party did not reverse Cardoso's sell-out. Indeed, Lula accepted his predecessor's neoliberal policies—embellished them—and set about forging an alliance between the Workers' Party and the economic elites, replacing Cardoso's Party! For the next few years, we were attacked by the Left academic and pundit world for having dared to advance such a critique on their 'worker president'! The consequences of what we had described as the PT's pact with the Right are clear to everyone today: Brazil is enmeshed in swindles, scandals and coups.

Introduction

> "The nature of the multitude is to arrive rapidly and depart swiftly".

For more than a decade, left-wing parties, accompanied by working class trade unions and landless rural social movements, dominated Brazil, the largest country in Latin America. Their political leaders were repeatedly elected; their trade union and rural social officials secured concessions from the state; the political process followed legal procedures adjudicating its agenda with the opposition business, banking and professional parties.

We were told the days of coups and revolutions were passed. Electoral processes, honest vote counts and mutual recognition of political legitimacy precluded any violent, dismissal and ouster of the established Left political leadership.

The Rise and Fall of the Political Left

The dominance of the Left is now only a memory! Its parties are in full retreat. Its leaders are scorned, insulted and prosecuted by their former political allies. The business allies of the past are now at their throats. Those politicians, who secured government positions in return for loyalty and votes, have fled clamoring for 'impeachment' and claiming deceit... while seeking new sources of patronage and plunder.

The great left political leaders, who had once bragged of 53 million voters, who were hailed in the international press for their command of a huge mass base while accommodating the interests of modern trade and business, are now condemned by the capitalist media as the cause of the current economic calamity.

The popular heroes of yesterday, who shared wealth and status with their rivals in the business elite, are now ostracized and facing show-trials for corruption.

The Trade Union and Rural Workers' Leaders

Veteran trade union and rural leaders came to the Presidential Palace to celebrate the electoral successes of the 'worker president'.

Once blushing with flattery, these mass leaders are now dismayed that the fiesta has ended and the music has stopped, while the workers and peasants are ordered to pay for the broken dishes and start the cleanup…

The mass popular organizations are now without allies in Congress; their voices are shut out of the bourgeois media; the domestic economy has been abandoned by the market; and the masses are in the streets clamoring for retribution against the politicians' betrayal. Now trade union and peasant leaders appeal for resistance and a return to class struggle, but their followers are in retreat!

Toward an Understanding of a Historical Defeat

The rise and fall of the Left is a historic reversal, which requires a systematic analysis of a disastrous strategy. The left's defeat cannot simply be dismissed as a betrayal by treacherous allies, corrupt party officials or plots concocted by billionaires and the US Embassy, leading up to a coup via a clearly phony impeachment process. The real question to ask is: Why did the Left allow such treachery and betrayal, culminating in a legislative coup d'état, to develop unopposed, leading to a reversal and rout of the Left? How could a huge multi-million-person voting machine, a vast and experienced trade union apparatus and a militant rural social movement fall, defeated without even a struggle?

The Strategy of the Left

The left parties deliberately adopted a short-term strategy of accommodation with the right, in part to avoid long-term, large-scale strategic confrontations with the defeated economic elite. For their part, the parties of the Right and their US advisors patiently chose to accept the Left's compromises and offers of cooperation, in order to prepare for a strategic offensive when the Left's mass support had declined.

The left parties embraced poorly thought-out 'short-cuts' to governance. They occupied government posts while cutting cozy deals with all the major power brokers of the Right.

The Left signed 'austerity' agreements with the IMF to restrain budgets and accept debt obligations. Members of notorious right wing and opportunistic political parties were brought into the cabinet, assigned strategic congressional leadership positions and placed on senior presidential advisory panels in exchange for their votes to approve loans, credits and regional development projects.

The Left negotiated deals with business elites, offering them generous subsidies and high profits, while restraining workers' demands for structural changes. They viewed this accommodation as an exchange for economic growth, wage increases and trade union recognition as a legitimate power sharer.

The Left dismissed the grassroots demands for social

transformation and they opposed any popular campaign to prosecute the financial elites for money laundering and white-collar crimes. Instead, they favored incremental increases in wages, poverty funds, pensions, and consumer credit.

The Left ignored the reality that such arrangements with the business elites were only a temporary truce rather than a permanent, strategic alliance.

The trade unions followed the lead of the left political leadership. They directed their mass organizations to accept negotiations based on periodic wage increases, more funds for trade union education, and subsidies for new union building complexes. The trade union leaders discouraged strikes, repressed demands for public ownership, and prevented any investigation into mining, banking, and agro-business corruption, tax evasions, and bribery. Even the well-documented wave of assassinations of landless worker activists and the naked land grabs of 'protected' Indian territories went unpunished.

The business elite realized they faced a potential radical mass movement, which was under the control of an elected 'left' government. They were 'delighted' that this left government was so willing to accommodate capitalist demands. They cautiously decided that short-term rewards and well-placed bribes would help prepare the ground for their restoration to power and reversal of the left's concessions.

The left rural social movements retained their radical socialist rhetoric and mass membership, but their leadership followed the left parties in government.

In exchange for subsidies to set up and expand community-based rural organizations and training schools for farmworkers, the social movements mobilized their mass activists to turn out the vote for the Left parties' President and Congress people.

The rural movement leaders justified their accommodation with the Left-business alliance by describing the Left regime as a 'field of contention', where they could press for radical changes. After more than a dozen years of successful mass struggle, the radical rural movement chose to ally with the left party apparatus! Only when the 'Left President' was impeached did the rural workers' leader call for the return to class struggle!

The Left's Short Term Gains and Long Term Losses

The political leaders on the left, as well as trade union and rural movement leaders, all believed they had a winning strategy. They claimed their mostly superficial gains were evidence of their success. Their successes included:

(1) Their governance for over four administrations where they increased or maintained the Left's voting majority.

(2) 'Pragmatic' political alliances with parties across the spectrum—won through various forms of bribery—as a formula for winning Congressional approval for major development contracts.

(3) Their funding of opposition allies, which attracted 'respectability' and enriched both Left politicians and their electoral campaigns.

(4) The decrease in social tension achieved by recruiting business opponents and gaining support among sectors of the capitalist class.

The left political leaders' strategy of accommodation depended on the economic success of the mineral-oil-agriculture export elites. This ignored the business sector's fundamental policy of cutting social and productive investments whenever markets, profits and economic opportunities declined.

When the left regime's public subsidies for the

export industry declined following the collapse of the global commodity market, the entire capitalist elite coalesced into a virulent right wing opposition.

When the previous political accommodation with capital, held together by corruption and questionable subsidies, became the target, the Right launched their strategic offensive.

The fact that business, banking, media and agro-mineral elites were able to join forces so quickly and launch their attack on the Left shows how they had flourished for a decade during the commodity boom.

The entire façade of a 'broad progressive coalition' disappeared. The trade union and rural movement structures linked to the left political leaders were incapable of mobilizing their mass base and countering the insurgent Right. For over ten years, the left regime had cut all its political deals in Congress, in the corridors of elite power, while ignoring class struggle.

This was a 'left' regime wholly dependent on market conditions and business allies. It was unable to defend any strategic ground when the Right regained its power base.

The left regime had retained an intact and fully functioning right administrative and judicial apparatus, composed of courts and judges, with the prosecutors and investigators all aligned with the Right opposition. They were ready to undermine the regime's congressional majority by opening 'corruption' investigations targeting the Left. Meanwhile, the business elite managed to intensify the consequences of the economic recession and insist that 'recovery' meant austerity against the poor.

The Right purchased its street crowds and mobilized its party allies, including the center, the fascists, the neo-militarists, the agro-business elite, and the imperial and local financial press. From Sao Paulo to New York to London, they were poised to forcibly oust the elected left President from power and jail its leaders.

Conclusion

The Left believed in the myth of democratic capitalism. They had faith that their negotiations with the business elites would increase social welfare. They operated on a platform of gradual accommodation of class interests leading to multi-class alliances and strategic conciliation between business and labor.

The historical lesson has proven otherwise—again. Business and the capitalist elite make clear, tactical short-term agreements in order to prepare a strategic counter-offensive. Their patient long-term strategy was to mobilize their class allies and overturn the electoral process—at the ripe moment.

The left parties depended on achieving a series of 'strategic understandings with the capitalist class' where both would benefit at a time of peak global demand for Brazil's commodities, instead of expanding their popular mandate by transforming the economy and domestic market.

The Left behaved as if favorable world market conditions would last forever. They lost their chance to use their 53 million-voter strength and radically change the organization and ownership of Brazil's strategic economic sectors!

In this way, the Left imitated the Right, choosing to share its power bases through accommodation with their business-partners. These were amateurs at the bourgeois power game, who found themselves entrapped in corruption and crisis! How shocking!

It was so much easier for the left politicians to get campaign funding through the usual practice of business payola than to campaign from door to door, factory to factory, village to village, fighting repression, elite media boycotts, and armed vigilantes.

In the end, their power base dissolved and their capitalist partners and political allies abandoned them: the left President was impeached.

Victorious capital and empire neatly ended this charade of market democracy. The retreating left parties begged for a reprieve via parliamentary vote and ended with a decisive defeat, bleating their last whimper as the door slammed shut...

Capitalists have never and will never recognize weak popular opposition. The capitalist political elite will always choose power and wealth over social democracy. The Left, in retreat, isolated and expelled from the corridors of power, now faces retribution from the most corrupt and treacherous of their former allies.

They usher in a lost generation.

Endnotes

1   James Petras, *Brazil and Lula: Year Zero*, Edifurb: Blumenau, Sao Paolo, 2005.
2   James Petras and Henry Veltmeyer, *Cardoso's Brazil: A Land for Sale*, Rowman and Littlefield, Lanham MD, 2003.

| Chapter Sixteen |

TWILIGHT OF THE IDOLS: RISE AND FALL OF THE PERSONALIST LEFT

Introduction

Over the past three years Latin American leftist leaders, who presided over heterodox 'free trade' and commodity-based welfare economies, lost presidential, legislative, and municipal elections and referendums or faced impeachment. They fell because they lost competitive elections, not because of US invasions or military coups. These same leftist leaders, who had successfully defeated coups and withstood gross US political intervention via USAID, NED, the DEA and other US government agencies, lost at the ballot box.

What accounts for the changing capacity of leftist presidents to retain majoritarian electoral support over almost a decade? Why did the US-backed and funded candidates win this time, when they had been defeated in several previous elections? What accounts for the defeat of the rightist violent road to power and their subsequent victory via the electoral process?

Class Struggle and Popular Mobilization as a Prelude to Leftist Electoral Victories

The electoral victories of the Left were preceded by a deep crisis in the 'free market' and deregulated economies, which were accompanied by intense class struggle from below. Class struggle polarized and radicalized vast sections of the working and middle classes.

In Argentina, the total collapse of the financial and manufacturing system led to a popular uprising and the rapid overthrow of three presidents. In Bolivia, two popular uprisings overthrew two US backed free market presidents. In Ecuador, a popular citizens movement ousted a US-backed president.

In Brazil, Paraguay and Venezuela, burgeoning peasant and urban movements, engaged in direct action and in opposition to their free market presidents, resulted in the election of left presidents.

Four interconnected factors came to the fore to explain the Left's rise to power: First, the dramatic collapse and ensuing socio-economic crisis, entailing poverty, stagnation and repression by right wing regimes, precipitated a large-scale shift to the left. Secondly, the intense class struggle, responding to the crisis, politicized the workers, radicalized the downwardly mobile middle classes, and eroded the influence of the ruling class and the impact of their elite-controlled mass media. Thirdly, the leftist presidents promised long-term, large-scale structural changes and successfully implemented immediate social impact programs (employment, social benefits, bank deposit protection, pay raises and large scale public investments). Last, but not least, the leftist presidents came to power at the beginning of or during a mega-cycle commodity boom providing multi-billion dollar surpluses in export earnings and tax revenues with which to finance new inclusionary social programs.

Electoral Clientalized Politics, Social De-Mobilization and Extractive Partnerships

During the first years of the left governments, they kept the heat on the right wing elites: defeating abortive coups, expelling intrusive US Ambassadors and US agencies, and defeating the local US clients.

They moved on the legal front to consolidate political power by convoking constitutional assemblies to approve progressive constitutions. They attracted and built on the support from their new indigenous, popular, and middle class constituents.

The constitutional changes reorganized new social alignments, especially by taking into account the rights of indigenous people, but fell far short of serving as the basis for a change of property relations.

The left governments reinforced their dependence on agro-mineral exports by designing a growth strategy based on economic partnership with multinationals and agro-business plantation owners.

The rising prices of commodities on the world market led to increases in government revenues, public investment in infrastructure, and expanded employment in the public sector. The left governments constructed large-scale patronage systems and clientelistic electoral machines, which mobilized the masses on electoral and ceremonial occasions and for international forums.

International left academics and journalists were impressed by the left administrations' fiery rhetoric supporting anti-imperialist, anti-neoliberal policies. Local and overseas pundits parroted the rhetoric about new forms of socialism, 21st century socialism in Ecuador and Venezuela, and Andean socialism in Bolivia.

In actual practice long-term, large-scale contracts were signed with international giants like Repsol, Monsanto, Jindel, and scores of other imperial backed multinationals.

Big agro-exporters received credits, loans and technical aid while peasants and local producers received only the paper 'land titles' for their small holdings. No large-scale land distributions were undertaken. Landless peasants, who were engaged in land occupations, were forcibly evicted. Increased government spending on credit and technical assistance was channeled almost exclusively to large-scale soya, cattle, cotton, and other agro-exporters, which increased rural class inequalities and exacerbated the decline of food security.

During the decade, militants became functionaries, who developed ties with business groups and began their own process of social mobility.

The agro-mineral export model raised incomes and reduced poverty but also accentuated inequalities between government functionaries and peasants and urban workers. The newly affluent, upwardly mobile middle class no longer flocked to hear egalitarian rhetoric. They sought security, pursued credit-financed consumerism, and looked upward toward the wealthy elite for their role models and life style changes rather than expressing solidarity with those left behind.

From Retreat to Defeat: Pragmatic Accommodation as a Formula for Neoliberal Restoration

The leaders' anti-imperialist rhetoric was increasingly discounted by most people as it was contrasted with the large-scale inflow of capital and the contracts with multinationals. The symbolic gestures and local projects celebrated before large crowds were accepted but increasingly failed to compensate for the daily routines of centralized power and local corruption.

Over the decade the political cadres of the left governments rounded-up votes via electoral patronage favors, financed by bribes from contractors and illicit transfers of public funds. Re-election bred complacency, arrogance, and a sense of impunity. The perquisites of office were taken for granted by party leaders but were perceived as unwarranted privileges by many working class and peasant voters. The de-radicalization process at the top and middle levels of the left regimes led the lower classes to rely on individualistic, family, and local solutions to their everyday problems.

With the demise of the commodity cycle, the broad coalition of workers, peasants, middle class, and professional groups splintered. Many rejected the malfeasance of the left regimes as a betrayal of the promise of change.

Thus the popular sectors embraced the moralizing critique mounted by the right. The retrograde radical right exploited discontent with the incumbents and played down or disguised their plans to reverse and undermine the employment and salary gains, pensions and family allowance gained over the decade.

Conclusion

The left governments stimulated the growth of extractive capitalism and converted their mass base into a passive recipient of regime reforms. The unequal power between leaders and followers was tolerated as long as the incremental rewards continued to flow.

As classes rose in the social hierarchy they shed their leftist ideology borne of crisis and looked to elite politicians as the new 'modernizers'.

The left regimes encouraged a dependency culture in which they competed for votes on the bases of growth, markets, and patronage.

The left functionaries, unable to rise via the closed agro-mineral sectors under the control of the multinationals, turned to state corruption, extracting commissions as intermediaries for the MNC, or simply absconding with public funds allocated for municipal health, education and infrastructure projects.

As a result, electoral promises were not kept. The corrupt practices were ignored by their elected leaders, deeply offending the popular electorate, who were disgusted by the spectacle of corrupt left politicians applauding radical rhetoric while raiding federal funds with impunity.

Party loyalty undermined any national political oversight of local politicians and functionaries. Disenchantment with the local functionaries spread up to the top. Popular leaders, who were repeatedly elected, soon were implicated or at least complicit in bribe-taking.

The end of the decade and the end of the commodity boom marked the twilight of the idols. The Left lost elections throughout the region.

Epilogue

The Kirchner-Fernandez regime was defeated in Argentina (2015).

The Lula-Rousseff regime faces indictment and impeachment in Brazil (2014-2016).

The Chavez-Maduro regime lost the legislative election in Venezuela (2015).

The Evo Morales regime lost the constitutional amendment allowing the president's third term re-election in Bolivia (2016).

| Chapter Seventeen |

PAST AND PRESENT ISLAMIST, DEMOCRATIC AND NAZI INTERNATONAL BRIGADES

Introduction

The Islamic State (IS) has become a magnet for international brigades, drawing over 30,000 fighters from 5 continents and 86 countries to their war in Iraq and Syria.

While the international brigades are part of a global movement, most of the volunteers come from two dozen countries, mainly in the Middle East, Maghreb, Western Europe, Russia, and Central Asia.

Most Islamist internationalists are paid a salary to fight and engage in police functions within IS-occupied regions.

This chapter will identify the principal sources of recruitment of Islamist internationalists and the reasons underlying their commitment. We will also contrast and compare IS internationalists to the earlier international brigades fighting for the Spanish Republic against fascists in the 1930s; fascist internationalists fighting for the Nazis against the USSR in the 1940s; and the democratic internationalists in the 1970s who joined the Sandinista revolution against the Somoza dictatorship.

Comparing IS to Past Internationalists

The IS 'volunteers' most closely resemble the Nazi internationalists in the substance and style of their politics. Both fused rabid religion in their fight against 'godless atheism and communism', as did the Ukrainian volunteers who collaborated with the Nazi armies invading the USSR. IS uses similar slogans in its attacks against secular Syria and Westernized Iraq. Both the Nazi volunteers and IS fighters are financed by established right wing regimes: in the past by Hitler's Germany and today by Saudi Arabia, the US, and Turkey.

In contrast the international brigades that fought for the Spanish Republic were mostly secular democrats, socialists, and communists, who received some arms from the USSR and limited financial aid from leftist individuals and organizations in the Western capitalist democracies.

The internationalists who went to Nicaragua to join with the Sandinista struggle against the Somoza dictatorship were mostly Latin Americans, with a sprinkling of Europeans and North Americans. Most of the volunteers were from Central America (El Salvador, Panama and Costa Rica) as well as political refugees who had fled the brutal military takeovers in Chile, Argentina, and Uruguay. The conflict pitted internationalists who were anti-imperialist, democrats, socialists, and supporters of liberation theology against a US-backed oligarchical dictatorship monopolizing the land, wealth, and power.

The Sandinistas, like the IS, opposed US dominance, but clearly differed in their tactics, allies, and strategic goals. The internationalist volunteers in Nicaragua fought for a secular, democratic, socialist government with close ties to socialist Cuba. IS retains ideological similarities to the Salafist orientation of Saudi Arabia and is funded by wealthy Saudis (though along with the US, the absolutist Saudi monarchy first facilitated it then lost control over it, and now fears it) and to the authoritarian but democratically elected Islamist regime of Recep Erdogan of Turkey.

The IS internationalists engage in generalized terror, mass murder, and destruction of historic and symbolic sites in conquered towns, cities, and villages in furtherance of their ideological orientation. Likewise the pro-Nazi internationalists in Ukraine and the Baltic States and elsewhere had imposed a regime of terror, murdering ideological enemies such as members of trade unions, cooperatives, as well as Jewish and leftist organizations.

A major difference between the Nazi collaborators and Islamist volunteers is found in the areas of action. Most of the Nazi internationalists engaged in terrorist activity overseas against their republican, democratic, and communist enemies. In contrast IS volunteers rotate from their home base to Iraq-Syria and return. According to one study up to 39% of the European jihadist internationalists go back to their home countries. Many continue to support and practice Islamist armed struggle. In contrast, the Spanish Republican and Nicaraguan internationalists of the 1930s and 1970s returned home to pursue democratic and socialist politics via elections and mass movements, where possible, and by arms where necessary (like in El Salvador).

In summary, whereas the internationalism of the earlier periods in the 20th Century reflected the polarization between left and right, between Hitlerian fascism and varieties of socialism, today left internationalism is in decline and right wing Islamist internationalism is on the rise.

According to recent studies the number of IS

volunteers has doubled between 2014 and 2015. Since 2011 over 30,000 overseas volunteers from 100 countries joined IS.[1]

The Growth Centers of IS Internationalists

The number of IS volunteers from Western Europe has doubled over the past year, to over 5,000. (In contrast the number from North America remains around 280 jihadists.) The number of IS volunteers from Russia and Central Asia has increased 300% reaching 4,700, of which 2,400 are from the Russian Federation (mostly Chechens and Dagestanis) and 2,100 are Turks and Kazaks.

The key centers of IS growth are found in the Middle East, where 8,240 fighters joined the terrorist army in Syria and Iraq. Other "hot spots" are the Gulf States, with 2,500 Saudis and more than 6,000 from the Maghreb, mostly Tunisians.

IS internationalists are increasing in direct proportion to the increasing military intervention of the US, EU, and Russia. The reasons for joining IS vary by country and cannot be subsumed under a single cause, whether it is religion, ethnicity, class, imperialism, or economic remuneration.

In many ways IS has become a magnet for global grievance-holders in a deteriorating world. Force and violence coming from the dominant Western countries has provoked a reciprocal response from a great variety of uprooted, deracinated, and educated classes. The IS war against the West is, in part, a convergence of Saudi billionaires experiencing vicarious holy wars and underworld semi-literate fighters from Europe's urban ghettos.

The IS is a multinational and national army, ruling by fiat, bound by a rigid hierarchical structure and Salafist ideology, which is transmitted through the use of sophisticated high-tech social media. Like the Israeli State, IS harnesses billionaires and high-tech innovations to religious textual justifications. IS draws economic support from various apparently contradictory forces: financial backing from oil sales via Turkey to Israel; billions from the Saudi regime at war with Shia and secular regimes and movements; arms from the US and EU seeking regime change in Bashar al-Assad's Syrian government.

IS and Washington's 'Coalition of 60'

Washington's claim that it leads a coalition of 60 governments against IS is deeply flawed because it is based on verbal commitments from regimes which, in practice, are actually working with the IS. Moreover, for many crucial US partners the fight against IS is a pretext for other political-military priorities.

A prime example is Turkey, which attacks and bombs the secular Kurds in Syria and Northern Iraq under the pretext of fighting IS. Ankara supplies 'volunteers', arms, training, financing, and sanctuaries to the IS. Erdogan's Turkomen proxies in Syria fight against Kurds as well as the government of Bashar al-Assad.

Saudi Arabia and the Gulf States provide 'volunteers,' finances, religious ideology, and arms to IS and other extremists groups to fight and defeat the Shia regime in Iraq, the secular government in Syria and the Houthis movement in Yemen—all the while claiming to be a member of the US coalition against IS.

Israel, which claims to oppose IS and Islamist terrorism, provides cross border medical care to IS fighters wounded in southern Syria and bombs the Syrian armed forces as they pursue IS fighters.

Worst of all, most of the IS arms come from the

US, either captured from retreating Iraqi armies or received directly from so-called moderate rebels who either sell them to or join the jihadis, handing over their US arms to IS.

Like the Nazi international brigades, IS internationalists have powerful state backers who wage phony wars in a game of mutual manipulation. The Saudis export their domestic extremists to Syria and Iraq, seeking to safeguard the absolutist monarchy. The US and EU allowed IS volunteers to travel to Syria to overthrow the Bashar al-Assad government—and then exploited the returnees' links to terrorism to strengthen the domestic police state. Turkey promotes IS to prevent an autonomous Kurdish state in northern Syria and to expand its southern border by annexing a band of Syrian territory.

Russia, Iran, and Hezbollah, which were invited by the Damascus government to fight against IS, are seriously engaged in the war against IS. They fear an IS conquest of Syria will result in a launch-pad for terrorists returning to their countries. Chechens and Dagestani fighters among the IS jihadis receive arms, training and financing, and are committed to return to Russia to apply the terror they learned in Syria and Iraq.

Turkey's aggression and attack against Russia—including the shooting down of a Russian jet which had been bombing IS oil convoys heading for Turkey and Ankara's proxies among the Turkomen—is indicative of its powerful links to IS.

Conclusion

The formal and informal international organization of Islamist extremists, led and inspired by IS, has encouraged tens of thousands of volunteers from dozens of countries in five continents. These international brigades are recruited on the basis of various appeals—not merely religious, but with personal, political and monetary appeals. Many go abroad to Syria and Iraq to secure training with the intention of returning to engage in armed attacks in their country of origin. Their strength is not so much in their numbers or commitment but in the powerful support they receive from major powers in the region and the world. If it was not for Turkey, they would not be able to enter Syria nor receive pay or arms resulting from IS oil sales via the Erdogan connection. The volunteers would not advance in battle if it were not for US arms captured or bought from Iraqi arms depots and those supplied by the US to its Syrian 'moderate rebels'. Wounded IS volunteers would not return to battle if it were not for Israeli medical care.

Many IS volunteers would not fight under the banner of Wahhabi extremism if the Saudi Arabians did not pay their salaries and buy their arms. In other words, IS 'internationalism' is largely state-sponsored, dependent on the interests and strategic needs of global and regional powers.

In contrast the internationalists who fought on the side of the Spanish democratic Republic (1936-39) against fascist Franco and great regional powers (Germany and Italy) were not supported by the US, Great Britain, France, etc.

Likewise, the internationalists who fought with the Nicaraguan Sandinistas against the Somoza dictatorship, fought against the Great Powers—mainly the US—and received marginal support from Cuba and Panama.

The internationalism and the justice of the cause for IS is discredited by the backers of their struggle. The current IS-led movement is backed by regional and global imperial powers intent on using international volunteers as cannon fodder for their imperial goals, which include destroying independent governments, establishing client regimes, seizing economic resources, and expanding territory in order to establish military bases surrounding global and regional rivals, Russia, Iran, and China.

Endnotes

1 "Up to 30,000 Fighters Have Gone to Syria / Iraq since 2011—Report," *The Guardian,* November 17, 2015 <https://www.theguardian.com/world/2015/nov/17/30000-foreign-fighters-syria--iraq-2014-terrorism-report>

PART FOUR

ZIONISM IN AMERICA

| Chapter Eighteen |

ZIONIST POWER: SWINDLERS AND IMPUNITY, TRAITORS AND PARDONS

"We work so hard to establish ourselves and to get where we are and to have somebody [Jonathan Pollard] screw it up... and then have Jewish organizations line up behind this guy and try to make him out a hero of the Jewish people, it bothers the hell out of me..."
Admiral Sumner Shapiro,
US Navy Rear Admiral, former Director of the Office of Naval Intelligence (1978-82)[1]

"We... feel obligated to go on record with the facts regarding Pollard in order to dispel the myths that have arisen from the clever public relations campaign... aiming at transforming Pollard from greedy, arrogant betrayer of the American national trust into Pollard committed Israeli patriot"
Sumner Shapiro, William Studeman, John Butts and Thomas Brooks, former Directors of Naval Intelligence[2]

Introduction

Over two decades ago, Harvard political science professor, Samuel Huntington, argued that global politics would be defined by a 'clash of civilizations'. His theories have found some of the most aggressive advocates among militant Zionists, inside Israel and abroad.

Over the past decade, thousands of Palestinians have been slaughtered and wounded in the West Bank, Gaza, and Israel. The Israeli state terrorists, who commit mass murder in Palestine, are part of a movement that sees an inevitable mortal final battle between Zionism and the Muslim and Western world.

Many Western democratic leaders have questioned Huntington's prognosis and discreetly refuted the Zionist belief that different faiths and cultures cannot live and work together.

In the aftermath of the Paris attacks, leading Western Zionist ideologues have argued that, while liberal values should be reaffirmed, the US and EU leaders must recognize 'malign global Islamic trends'. Influential Western Zionist journalists and ideologues, who dominate the mass media, argue that 'hardline Islamism' is on the rise, even in previously moderate Muslim countries like Turkey, Malaysia and Bangladesh ... However, these ideologues (for example Gideon Rachman of the *Financial Times*) systematically avoid commenting on the rise of hardline Zionism in its most racist form in Israel and the conversion of formerly moderate Zionist organizations into willing accomplices of Israeli state terror against a captive people.

Together, these developments in Israel and among the major Zionist organizations in the US and the European Union have limited the space for critics of the 'clash of civilizations' dogma.

State terror assaults, such as those taking place daily in Palestine, incite tensions between Zionists and non-Zionists—and that is their intent. Larger structural and systemic forces are at work and are driving Zionist radicalization. One of the most pernicious is the way in which wealthy US and EU Zionist individuals and organizations, in particular the Presidents of the 52 Major American Jewish Organizations, have used their economic power to spread the most intolerant forms of Judaism into the rest of the Western World.

The effects are now visible in the major political institutions and media of the US, England and the Continent. Previously, France was held up as an example of a successful multi-cultural nation—a dubious assumption as any historian of colonial France can testify. But that image is rapidly changing. Influential Zionists have fomented widespread Islamophobia and authored legislation restricting free speech in France which has outlawed criticism of Israel as 'anti-Semitism'.

French civil libertarians have noted that political and social space has increasingly narrowed for 'non-Zionists', especially for anyone critical of Israel's state terrorism. In other words, there is immense pressure in France to 'keep quiet' or self-censor in the face of Zionist racist brutality—so much for Les Droits de l'Homme et du Citoyen.

For over a decade, Zionist influence, especially from Israel's far-right Netanyahu regime, has eroded the French version of 'moderate Zionism', replacing it with a more doctrinaire, exclusivist and authoritarian version. Worldwide condemnation of Israel's massacre during the 2008-9 Operation Cast Lead of over 4,000 entrapped Palestinians in Gaza, the world largest prison camp, led the Netanyahu regime to resort to a virulent Zionist version of 'identity politics' to rally support for the slaughter—or enforce silence among the horrified. Numerous prestigious rabbis have blessed the killing of unarmed Palestinians. A prominent Israeli jurist, Justice Minister Ayelet Shaked, urged the killing of Arab women so they would not give birth to 'little snakes'. Israeli-Jewish judges have exonerated IDF soldiers, police and settlers for killing Palestinian children—even unarmed teenaged Arab girls hysterical over their brutal humiliation. And world public opinion is ordered to 'move along, look away, nothing for you to see here...' Meanwhile, Israeli Cabinet ministers denounced US President Obama and Secretary of State Kerry as 'anti-Semites' for their administration's negotiations over Iran.

All the major overseas Jewish organizations have marched in step. In the United States, a country with a democratic constitution and centuries-old Bill of Rights, self-styled 'mainstream Zionists' have defended Israeli spies and criminals, as well as un-extraditable swindlers, and organized nationwide networks of university, professional, and business organizations to demand the firing of colleagues and to suppress free speech and free assembly of Israel's critics.

Major Zionist organizations and leaders are first and foremost in stoking the fire of anti-Muslim and anti-Arab racist rhetoric, which has now become commonplace in the mass media and among Republican candidates engaged in the current Presidential nomination campaign.

The convergence of these developments in Israel and among the Zionist power configuration in North America, Europe and the Middle East is resurrecting Huntington's decades-old idea of a 'clash of civilizations'.

Ironically, the ideological marriage of Herzl and Huntington is also fast eroding the former reality of Jewish and non-Jewish integration and intermingling across the globe. The alternative to pluralist civilizations is more primitive and brutal injustice, violence and death.

Contemporary Manifestations of Zionist Power in the US: The Release of the Most Damaging Spy-Traitor in US History

On November 20, 2015, former Naval Intelligence Analyst, Jonathan Pollard, the American-Jewish spy for Israel, was freed by the Obama regime under Zionist pressure after repeated refusals by three Republican and one Democratic President and over the objections of the heads of all 27 major US intelligence agencies. The significance of this release has to be viewed against the history of Pollard's crimes.

Fabricating Lies to Justify Obama's Release of Pollard
The mass media and the 52 Presidents of the Major American Jewish Organizations (AIPAC, ADL, etc…), claim that:

1) Pollard committed espionage against US security for 'altruistic reasons'—a deep concern for Israel's security and because US intelligence agencies had refused to share crucial information with Israel's intelligence counterparts (out of anti-Semitism);

2) the information Pollard handed over had no lasting harm and did not endanger US security; and

3) Pollard's punishment was 'excessive', his 'repentance' was sincere and his example precluded any future Israeli espionage activity against the US.

These assertions are completely false.

Pollard was a mercenary, spying against the US out of greed. He lived a decadent, expensive lifestyle and had demanded the Israelis pay him a total package of over $250,000 for his work. The Israeli Embassy was known to have paid Pollard, a US Naval Analyst, to spy against the United States government. Court records reveal that he collected over $50,000 for 'expenses' during his espionage career, including expensive jewelry, and a monthly stipend of $2500. Court records furthermore reveal that he offered to sell additional secret documents to Pakistan, Apartheid South Africa, Australia, Russia, and some Middle East countries.

He collected dozens of box-loads of confidential documents, many of which had nothing to do with the security of Israel, but were deemed essential to US global security, including a top secret ten-volume set of National Security Agency high level codes exposing the most advanced means and methods of espionage and the main targets of intelligence collection. Some of his 'vacuumed-up' treasure trove included the identity of US intelligence operatives and assets in Warsaw Pact countries and the Soviet Union.

The 17 US intelligence agencies have consistently opposed Pollard's release because his sale of this information to the Israelis led to the capture and execution of US operatives after Israel handed over this top-secret information to the Soviet Union in exchange for allowing Soviet Jews to immigrate to Israel in massive numbers. Needless to say, this treason crippled US intelligence operations and led to deaths. US military and intelligence officials view Pollard as having 'blood on his hands'. So much for the 'altruistic American Zionist keen on helping Israel.' Years of Zionist propaganda and lobbying have obscured this aspect of Pollard's crimes.

Excessive Punishment or Excessive Leniency?

Far-right Israeli Cabinet Ministers and liberal American Jews, supporters and opponents of Pollard, pundits and editorialists, argue that the sentence of life imprisonment given to Pollard was out of proportion to the crime of treason. They claim that, after 30 years, he was 'overdue' for release.

The severity of the punishment is determined by the crime and the damage caused. In cases of treason and espionage committed by US officials (especially for money), the sentence is always severe. The leaders of the John Anthony Walker Naval spy ring were given multiple life sentences in 1985 and there are many other similar cases.

Among the documents Pollard handed over to his Israeli handlers (operating out of the Israeli Embassy), was US intelligence on strategic installations in Syria, Lebanon and Iraq. No doubt, this provided Israel with strategic coordinates to bomb major security facilities in those countries as well as facilitated their brutal invasion and occupation of Lebanon in the 1980s. Pollard's treachery led to the death of thousands of civilian lives in Lebanon and facilitated the wars in Iraq and Syria. The damage to those countries and to innocent people would not have been considered by the judge in Pollard's life sentence—but it must be considered here, in understanding the enormity of his crimes. Pollard has boasted that he was operating out of a 'racial imperative' to protect Israel.

While in prison Pollard became an Israeli citizen, a salaried officer in the Israeli armed forces and, after divorcing his American wife (who had also engaged in espionage for pay and served several years in prison), he re-married a Canadian-Israeli woman. This sheds a different light on the severity of his life sentence for treason.

Pollard did not serve out this 'life sentence'. He was paroled in November 2015 (to the cheers of his adoring Jewish-American fans) demonstrating the wealth and power of American Zionists and their ability to buy the support of US politicians, domestic and foreign notables and the entire Israeli-Jewish political spectrum—and push aside the objections of the heads of the three major US armed services and US intelligence agencies.

Israeli public opinion overwhelmingly supports Pollard and regards him as a 'role model' for other US Zionists in official positions. Contrary to Israeli lies, several other major Israeli spy operations occurred in the US after Pollard, including the case involving AIPAC officials, Rosen and Weissman, and Pentagon analyst Larry Franklin during George W. Bush's administration.

In stark contrast to the freeing of an Israeli spy responsible for endangering the security of thousands of US operatives abroad and millions of innocent civilians, two authentic American political prisoners, who have fought for the rights of minorities, rot in jail with no prospect of freedom. Leonard Peltier, a Native American leader, has spent 38 years in the highest security prison and Mumia Abu-Jamal, an African-American leader from Philadelphia, has spent 33 years on death row or brutal solitary confinement. Both were framed by perjured evidence in a parody of justice, which has revolted and generated ongoing support from millions around the world. Neither threatened US security. Over the years, numerous witnesses, legal authorities, and academics have testified regarding the miscarriage of justice that characterized their 'show trials' and have pleaded for their humanitarian release.

Unlike Pollard, and despite decades of worldwide campaigns for their release, Peltier and Abu-Jamal will probably die entombed in prison. Unlike Pollard, their cases were never about treason, selling information, and greed. They have worked and continue to work hard for justice within their communities, hence earning the hatred of the police state. They fought to serve their oppressed American communities, unlike Pollard who is purported to have served an oppressive and racist Israeli elite determined to oppress and erase the native Palestinian population.

The decisive factor has been the political power of

Pollard's supporters, the US Zionist Power Configuration, which leads President Obama and 430 US members of Congress (to quote Ariel Sharon)... 'by the nose!' Through their media connections, they can lie about Pollard's case and his motives. They can minimize the consequences of his treason and twist the arms of obedient politicians to support a traitor. Despite the fact that scores of high-ranking US intelligence and military officials have repeatedly attested to the damage inflicted by Pollard on the US, campaign-finance-hungry politicians recite the Zionist line that Pollard's treason did not warrant a harsh sentence!

Beyond the immediate shame of a US president caving in to Israeli pressure with regard to this spy, there is the issue of the flagrant double standard: Why do Israeli spies (or American Zionist traitors) evoke the unconditional support of the entire US Zionist apparatus?

Why do thousands of rabbis, hundreds of movie executives and media moguls, and scores of billionaires (talk about the 0.01%!) campaign on behalf of this arrogant, greedy thief?

Why does Pollard merit a totally different standard of justice, in stark contrast to the vast majority of American minorities, who can rot in dungeons even when clearly innocent?

Why does a self-described Israeli (who renounced his US citizenship while in jail), who sold vital national secrets to fund a decadent life-style and for what he described as a 'race imperative,' merit such favors while hundreds of thousands of poor US citizens are routinely denied leniency—let alone mercy?

Clearly, the interests of Israel, a foreign regime, carry much greater weight within the US judicial system than millions of American minorities...

Cyber Crimes of Our Times: Billionaire Israeli Swindlers and the Chinese Military

For over three years, the Obama administration, the NSA and the Secretary of Defense, Ashton Carter have fed their media mouthpieces breathless denunciations against China for cyber-theft. Every week, there are lurid stories about the theft of confidential US industrial, military, and political intelligence committed by the Chinese. The Obama regime has followed up his charges of 'cyber theft' by threatening to confront China in the South China Sea, apply sanctions, and raise the military ante in the Pacific against the world's most dynamic economic superpower.

Assistant Secretary of State Victoria Nuland (Nudelman-Kaplan) has claimed that Chinese cyber theft is a top national security threat requiring an immediate military-security response. US officials have provided no evidence that Chinese officials, at any level, are involved in espionage. Moreover they have presented no proof that cyber theft is a policy of the Chinese government! There has been no evidence that these alleged thefts have damaged US companies or security interests. Nevertheless US hostility toward China has been justified by unproven accusations which are used to increase the possibility of a major confrontation.

Contrasted with the 'allegations' against the Chinese, three 'Israeli businessmen' have been officially charged by US prosecutors with running a multi-billion dollar cyber-hacking scam within the US over the past 5 years. Dubbed the biggest financial hack in US history, the story hardly made headlines in the US media and was conveniently buried by subsequent 'terror attacks' in Europe.

The case is instructive. Three Israelis (one a US-Israeli dual citizen) hacked-attacked ten of the largest US financial institutions, including JP Morgan Chase and Fidelity Investments, as well as the *Wall Street Journal*, downloading protected information on over 100 million Americans—the biggest hack-attack in US history. Gery Shalon, Ziv Orenstein, and Joshua Samuel Aaron employed hundreds of employees in Israel and elsewhere, running a mega-cybercriminal enterprise.

According to the *Financial Times*, "the hacks took place from 2012 to mid-2015 and were aimed at aiding stock market manipulation that generated tens of millions of dollars."[3] In addition to selling 'pumped-up' stocks to millions of customers of the companies they had hacked, Shalom *et al* launched cyberattacks to launder millions (more likely billions) for illegal drug and counterfeit software dealers, malicious malware distributors, illegal online casinos, and an illegal 'bitcoin exchange' known as 'Coin.mx.' Someone within the financial security apparatus of the US government (white collar crime unit) must have tipped them off. They are safe in Israel; the Netanyahu regime has yet to act on a US extradition order, although they are reportedly under 'house arrest' in their villas.

In contrast to the ongoing bellicose rhetoric, which Washington has directed against China's alleged hackers, Washington has been very reluctant to press the issue of extraditing the cyber-thieves with its special partner in Tel Aviv.

Israeli super-hackers' virulent attacks against major US financial institutions and American investors with apparent impunity followed the practice of Israeli info-tech operatives who have raided US military, technology and industrial sites for years.

While the US sends air squadrons and an armada of warships to Chinese waters over a few sand-bars, and brays about arresting Chinese researchers (whom it later released with no charges) for alleged cyber-theft, it cannot persuade its 'closest strategic ally', Israel, to hand over a trio of formally charged swindlers. Instead, the US increased its annual $3 billion in military aid to Israel and provides an open market for Israeli security products based on stolen US technology!

The reason for the differential response is not the nature of the crimes—it is *who commits the crimes*! Israeli dominance in US politics via the unconditional support of its US Zionist power configuration ensures impunity for Israeli citizens, including the ability to delay or postpone the extradition of notorious multi-billion-dollar cyber thieves! Washington feels free to accuse China, without proof of official Chinese complicity, despite overwhelming evidence, while it cannot persuade its close 'friend' Israel to extradite criminals. Netanyahu, backed by his Israeli-Jewish public will decide if, when and where to extradite. When it comes to shielding Israeli or American-Israeli criminals from American justice, Israel treats its ally in Washington like an enemy.

Zionist political clout is evident in Washington's judicial leniency toward other mega-swindlers with ties to Israel. Michael Milken contributed millions of (swindled) dollars to Israeli and US Zionist programs and won a 'get out of jail' card despite his conviction for major financial scams. He served 2 years out of a 10-year sentence and was granted a 'humanitarian release' because he was 'dying' of extensive terminal metastatic prostate cancer. So far, Michael's quarter century of miraculous remission from 'terminal metastatic prostate cancer' constitutes a first in the annals of urologic cancer! He has gone on to re-constitute his fortune and prominence, while welfare mothers who took a few extra dollars rot in jail.

Ivan Boesky, another uber-Zionist and mega-donor

to Israel was a swindler of gargantuan proportions. He raked in hundreds of millions a year. He was tried, convicted and sentenced to a mere 42 months in prison. He was out in less than 24 months, thanks to the support of ....

Marc Rich, a mega-billionaire rogue trader who broke US sanctions against trading with enemies, was also a self-described agent for the Israeli Mossad. Despite having been convicted in absentia in US courts for fraud, (he had skipped bail for Switzerland), President 'Bill' Clinton pardoned the absentee felon in absentia—a historical first for a criminal who had never spent a day in the jail. Mrs. Rich's $100,000 donation to the Hillary Clinton's New York senatorial campaign probably did little to influence the President's sense of mercy.....

However, 'Bernie' Madoff, a $50 billion dollar swindler who gave huge amounts of illicit earnings to Zionist charities and projects in Israel was convicted and sentenced to over 100 years in prison. Unlike the above mentioned 'untouchables', Madoff will never breathe free again because he made the unforgivable mistake of mostly swindling other Jews, ardent Zionists, and even ripping off a number of pro-Israel foundations. His differential treatment stems from his poor choice of victims rather than his crimes. Otherwise he might now be enjoying a comfortable villa in Israel rather than a cold cell in Pennsylvania.

Conclusions

Israeli capacity to manipulate and influence the American judicial process is based on 52 powerful front organizations organized as the Presidents of the Major American Jewish Organizations.[4] Zionist officials and allies occupy strategic position within the White House and judiciary. This situation has made a mockery of the American court system and feeds the cynicism and bitterness of the average American.

Through their influence in the mass media, Zionist officials and their allies have converted a grotesque mercenary spy, like Jonathan Pollard, into an altruistic, Israeli-Jewish patriot, celebrated throughout Israel and within US Zionist circles. Veteran American intelligence and military official who opposed his release have been painted with the broad brush of 'anti-Semites'. The formidable Zionist power configuration, nurtured and financed by mega-swindlers, successfully secured his release. Zionist dominance essentially guarantees that the US will treat an indicted Israeli cyber-thief with extreme tact, supplicating the Israeli government for their extradition, while going ballistic over an alleged Chinese hacker.

Few progressive websites or even the micro-Marxist journals confront these issues, more out of moral cowardice (self-censorship) than ignorance. Instead they bleat general clichés and radical rhetoric about US imperialism and the rise of the right without identifying the precise social and political identity of the forces who move national policy. In a word, the Zionist Power Configuration gets more than a free ride.

Endnotes

1   *Washington Post*, June 16, 2008
2   Cited in Ronald Olive, *Capturing Jonathan Pollard: How one of the Most Notorious Spies in American History Was Brought to Justice*, Annapolis Maryland: Naval Institute Press, p. 248.
3   *Financial Times* (11/11/2015, p1)
4   The clout of the pro-Israel lobby has been documented in numerous previous works, see inter alia, *The Power of Israel in the United States* (2006), *Zionism, Militarism and the Decine of US Power* (2008), Clarity Press, Atlanta.

| Chapter Nineteen |

THE JEWISH POLICY ELITE IN THE UNITED STATES: MERITOCRACY, MYTH AND POWER

Introduction

Obama's nomination of Merrick Garland to the Supreme Court marks a continuation and deepening of the lopsided ethno-religious representation in the US judicial system. If Garland is appointed, the then four Jewish justices will comprise 45% of the Court, even though Jews represent less than 2% of the overall population. Roman Catholics comprise the other 55% of the Court, even though they represent approximately 30% of the population. Protestants, yes, WASPS (historically the authors and signers of the country's foundational documents, and the major confessional group) are totally absent from this august body of jurists.

Equally important, the power of Jewish justices on the Supreme Court is accelerating: counting Garland, two of the last three appointments (67%) have been Jews.

In the first half of the 20th century in the US,

progressive Jews and civil libertarians decried what they termed WASP (white Anglo-Saxon Protestant) exclusivity, privilege and discrimination, citing their domination of the Supreme Court and their 'over-representation' throughout the elite centers of power. Having totally displaced and replaced the dreaded WASPS, there is nary a word from the plethora of civil rights groups and Jewish organizations claiming to be concerned with issues of discrimination and exclusion. Perhaps the marginalized WASP population lacks any qualified jurists among their scores of millions, an ethno-cultural degeneration unique in US history? Or perhaps the last few WASPs appointed to the Supreme Court turned out to be among the most ardent and independent defenders of citizen rights, to the chagrin of numerous Administrations.

Nevertheless, if a rare individual should dare to raise the issue of nepotism and the exercise of narrow political considerations in the choice of Supreme Court nominees, the factious response is that 'it's all about merit'. Meaning, among the thousands of WASP graduates of the top law schools with academic awards and publications in prestigious journals, no qualified candidate could be found to address this lack of representation.

But scholarship and originality may not be of much merit: A brief perusal of the legal publications of Supreme Court Justice Elena Kagan and Supreme Court nominee Merrick Garland reveals meager, mediocre and pedestrian articles and monographs. In the case of Kagan, her rise to power was facilitated by her relationship with the former (and heartily voted out of office) Harvard President 'Larry' Summers, who appointed her Dean of the Law School despite her lack of quality publications. Summers, as Harvard President, led a raucous and bullying campaign against any academic critics of Israeli policies during his abruptly abbreviated tenure in office.

Clearly the problem of ethno-religious nepotism is not confined to Jews, it was an abuse practiced by WASP elites and others before them. Nor does such nepotism benefit the average wage and salaried Jews, who have to struggle side-by-side with their Gentile compatriots to make a living and exercise their rights.

However, nepotism or ethno-religious favoritism has become an acute problem now when exclusive control of the Supreme Court compounds the growing problems of abuse in other spheres of the power structure—political, economic and mass communications. This imbalance has profound repercussions on everything from US overseas wars of aggression to the everyday struggle of Americans faced with deepening inequalities and the shredding of the social contract.

Historically, and particularly among progressive and leftist critics, what was referred to as the "Jewish Problem" was a multifaceted issue that revolved around the persecution of resident Jews by anti-Semitic regimes and within Christian majority cultures. Various solutions included the granting of citizenship rights following the French Revolution, socio-cultural assimilation, the development of socialism or separation and re-settlement in Palestine through the Zionist movement. Today the major issue has turned into an 'American Problem': how to address the fact that a powerful ethno-religious elite can use its multi-faceted power to secure (and create) strategic positions in the state while excluding contenders, repressing critics and actively promoting policies in the interest of a foreign state, Israel.

Not all Jewish appointees and elected officials explicitly follow the extremist position of the most aggressive Zionist organizations, especially the self-styled Presidents of the Major American (sic) Jewish Organizations ... but nor do they openly object to Israeli-First activities or try to block them for fear of ostracism and retribution with the calumny of 'self-hating Jew' unlikely to promote one's career or social life.

The Myth of Meritocracy and the Practice of Mediocracy

To deal with the rise of Israel-First individuals to positions of power in the US, it is essential to analyze the all-pervasive claims of meritocracy—the argument that their influence is based on their 'universally acclaimed' achievements, intelligence, and superiority far beyond their elite rivals. The argument of 'unique merit' blends smoothly with traditional Talmudic and contemporary Israeli-chauvinist belief that Jews are 'the Chosen People of God', destined to prevail over the inferior 'others'.

The meritocratic argument is partly based on circular arguments contending that the disproportionate number of Jewish billionaires means they are more brilliant in business; that pro-Israel dominance within the US corporate mass media proves that Jewish media moguls are smarter and Israel is a righteous state; and the rise of Israel-Firsters in government, academia, and finance reflects their higher intelligence, greater work ethic, and accomplishments.

It is with the latter that we have to deal, because the significance of higher grades, diplomas from prestigious universities and piles of academic awards has to be proven. Furthermore, it is not simply the achievement of high individual positions and great wealth that matter, but how the policies formulated and practices pursued by these elite individual have affected the lives of 330 million Americans, the nation, its prestige, welfare, and moral authority.

If we use these alternative, evidence-based criteria, we find a huge disparity between high levels of academic achievement and disastrous performance when in public office.

We can cite the Federal Reserve chairman, Alan Greenspan, whose deregulatory policies led to the greatest financial crash since the Great Depression and his successor, Benjamin Bernanke, who presided over the trillion-dollar bailout of Wall Street banks while millions of American's lost their homes. Both attended elite institutions, both secured numerous prestigious awards... and both imposed disastrous policies on the American nation and people, with complete impunity for their monumental mistakes, while American workers continue to suffer.

Treasury Department

Stuart Levey was the first Undersecretary for Terrorism and Financial Intelligence within the US Treasury Department (a position created due to demand for it by AIPAC and tailored specifically for Levey). He graduated from Harvard College summa cum laude and magna cum laude. While Stu Levey was racing around the US and the rest of the world enforcing the economic sanctions against Iran (which he authored in line with Israeli directives), narco-terrorists from Mexico, Central America, Colombia and Peru were freely washing hundreds of billions of dollars a year in US banks. Meanwhile, Saudi Arabian officials who funded jihadi terrorists were never prosecuted or sanctioned—even after questions arose as to the engagement of some Saudis in financing some of the attackers within the US.

Levey's successor, David Cohen (who else!) followed the same policy. Multinational banks and corporations, which had corrupted officials, swindled investors, evaded taxes and laundered illicit funds were never investigated, let alone charged. Cohen devoted his time and effort, at Israel's behest, enforcing sanctions against Iran and endeavoring to sabotage any US-Iran nuclear negotiations.

Foreign Policy

From the Clinton era through the George W. Bush and Obama regimes, the US engaged in a series of wars against predominantly secular governments in Muslim countries, which had been opposed to Israel's brutal occupation of Palestine.

Key policymakers in the design and execution of US war policy were prominent Jews bristling with diplomas from the most prestigious universities.

These 'scholars', the 'cream' of US academe, blatantly falsified the pretexts for the US's disastrous thirteen-year war (and counting) in Iraq, the lost (15-plus year) war in Afghanistan, the invasion and destruction of Libya and Syria. Their brilliant plans have led directly to the rise of ISIS throughout the region and the displacement of tens of millions of civilians in the Middle East, West Asia and North Africa.

Due credit must be given to the midwives of the 21st century wars of foreign conquest and domestic decay: Standing out among the principal architects of these foreign policy disasters is Elliott Abrams, BA and Doctor of Jurisprudence, Harvard University. Abrams had been officially censored for directly lying to the US Congress about his role in the Iran-Contra scandal under President Ronald Reagan in the 1980s. During that administration, Elliot directed US official support for the dictatorial regimes in Nicaragua, Guatemala, El Salvador and Honduras where over 250,000 Central American civilians were massacred. The new millennium wiped clean his tawdry slate of crimes against humanity and he was appointed a leading National Security Advisor under President George W. Bush, 2002-2009. In this role, he fabricated evidence linking the secular government of Iraq to the fundamentalist Al Qaeda and he served as a transmission belt channeling false Israeli intelligence that Iraq possessed banned weapons of mass destruction. No weapons were ever found—a 'mere detail of history', according to his partner, Paul Wolfowitz. These blatant lies pushed the Bush administration to invade and destroy Iraq.

While Elliot Abrams was strategically placed in the Bush/Cheney White House, his partners in deception, Paul Wolfowitz and Douglas Feith controlled Middle East policy at the Pentagon. This dream team of Abrams, Wolfowitz and Feith formed the powerful Israel-First Troika responsible for the military policies which systematically destroyed Iraq's state apparatus, decimating its civil society, fragmenting the country, and precipitating gruesome ethno-religious wars and the rise of ISIS. This Troika has never been held responsible for the deaths of over one million Iraqis—but credit should be given to the 'meritorious'.

Dr. Paul Wolfowitz received his BA from Cornell and PhD from the University of Chicago. In the 1980s, early in his government career, he temporarily lost security clearance for having passed confidential documents to Israeli agents. Despite this 'youthful indiscretion' (or act of treason), Wolfowitz became Deputy Defense Secretary under President George W. Bush (2001-2005). In this position, he was one of the earliest and most forceful advocates for military interventions against Iraq, Syria, Iran, Lebanon, and Libya. He persuaded the American Congress and the Bush Administration that the invasions of Afghanistan and Iraq would be short and self-financing. He glowingly predicted that the wars would 'pay for themselves' in terms of looted natural resources and reconstruction contracts. In fact, the wars in Iraq and Afghanistan have cost tens of thousands of US military casualties, over a trillion dollars in military expenditures and they continue over 13 years (Iraq), and

15 years (Afghanistan) with no end in sight but completely devastated societies spewing millions of refugees and thousands of terrorists.

Equally luminous in academic credentials, the third of the 'Israel-First Troika', Douglas Feith received his BA from Harvard (magna cum laude), and JD (magna cum laude). He worked closely with Israeli intelligence officials fabricating out of whole cloth the myth of Saddam's quest for 'yellow cake' uranium to construct Iraqi nuclear weapons of mass destruction pushing the US into war against Iraq.

Feith set up a cozy nest at the Pentagon, the 'Office of Special Plans' (OSP), which served as a base of operations for Israeli operatives. One thoroughly disgusted former Pentagon official described the flow of Israeli officials in and out of OSP as resembling 'a brothel on Saturday night'.

One of Feith's crowning achievements was the destruction of the Iraqi Baath Party and administrative apparatus, which included the entire police force, the army and public administration, education, and even the huge public health system. Virtually all qualified Iraqi officials were either fired or 'disappeared'. The result was the total breakdown of essential services, the pillage of the national and historic patrimony and decimation of civil and secular Iraqi society. Even the most fabulous archeological treasures of Mesopotamia were destroyed or looted for American and European collectors. Feith's level of meddling and disastrous policies led the colorful US General Tommy Franks to describe the Harvard 'JD' as "the dumbest fucking guy on the planet".

Hovering on the periphery of the 'Troika' was the 'mysterious', veteran manipulator, Richard Perle. With his BA from the University of Southern California and MA from Princeton (and no military experience), Perle was qualified to push for serial US wars on Israel's behalf, starting with Iraq and moving on to all other countries which had traditionally supported the rights of the Palestinian people. He was a key member of the US Defense Policy Board under the Bush Administration and the front ideologue for invading Iraq. His second 'job' was strategic adviser to Israeli Prime Ministers Ariel Sharon and Benyamin Netanyahu. Perle pushed for US military intervention to effect regime change in Syria and Iran as well as Libya.

Beyond the warrior troika and shadowy Mr. Perle, there is Dr. Dennis Ross, who received his BA and PhD from UCLA, and taught at Harvard's Kennedy School of Government. Ross and fellow uber-Zionist, Martin Indyk, founded the American Israel Public Affairs Committee (AIPAC) the most influential lobby on Middle East policy and a virtual king-maker in Washington. Ross was President Bill Clinton's 'Middle East Coordinator', ensuring that Israel's land grabs in the Occupied Territories were unimpeded and indeed justified, and funded by the US taxpayer. His notoriety in promoting the brutal and illegal confiscation of Palestinian property earned him the title of 'Israel's lawyer,' even among his most pro-Israel colleagues.

Ross made sure that Israel would not be bound to the Camp David agreements even as President Clinton claimed them as his landmark achievement in diplomacy. AIPAC, under Ross and Indyk, lobbied long and hard for the US invasion of Iraq; it backed Israel's invasion of Lebanon and justified the expansion of apartheid-style 'Jews only' colonial settlements in the occupied Palestinian West Bank.

During the Obama presidency, Ross served as Special Adviser for the Persian Gulf and Southwest Asia to Secretary of State Hilary Clinton. In this capacity, he actively opposed diplomatic negotiations with the government of Iran or the Taliban in Afghanistan.

Ross' partner, Martin Indyk, received his PhD from

the Australian National University and served as Deputy Research Director and co-founder of AIPAC (1982-85). This, the most powerful lobby in Washington, operates exclusively as a political fifth column for the Israeli Foreign Office. Indyk was founding Director of the Washington Institute of Near East Policy (WINEP), a barnyard of ideological propagandists for Israel. When President Clinton appointed (the Australian, Israeli, US citizen) 'Marty' Indyk as US Ambassador to Israel, serious questions arose concerning his transfers of confidential documents to Israel. He thus became the first Ambassador to be stripped of security clearance. Israel Lobby pressures led to reinstated security clearance for Indyk who was subsequently named Assistant Secretary of State for Near Eastern Affairs. As a mouthpiece for Israel's interests, Indyk has pushed to 'contain' Iraq (through bombing) and Iran (through economic sanctions).

Throughout his career, Indyk sabotaged peace negotiation between Israel and Palestine, and he undermined any early diplomatic resolution of the Iraq-US conflict, which might have prevented the disastrous war. His meddling on Israel's behalf has cost the US treasury hundreds of billions of dollars in lost trade with Iran. Despite his clear record of service to Israel and disservice to the US, President Obama appointed Indyk as US (sic) Special Envoy for Israel-Palestine Negotiations (2013-2014). In this supposedly diplomatic role he failed to protect even one acre of Palestinian farmland among the hundreds seized by Israel for the illegal establishment of many 'Jews Only' enclaves the occupied West Bank.

Economic Policy: More Mediocrity, Less Meritocracy

Jack Lew, Secretary of the Treasury (2013-2016) heads an ethno-chauvinist quintet dictating US foreign and domestic economic policy (with Michael Froman, Chief

Trade Negotiator; 'Penny' Pritzer, Secretary of Commerce; Lawrence Summers, Director of the National Economic Council and Janet Yellen, head of the Federal Reserve Bank). Lew pushed policies favoring the wealthiest 1% along with his co-religionist Michael Froman, while millions of Americans were plunged into poverty and stagnation. Their policies include Free Trade Agreements in Europe, Asia and Latin America, which have led to the relocation of US MNCs overseas, and massive job losses at home, further deepening inequalities and degrading working conditions and wages. Recently, in his stellar public career, Jack Lew was investigated for lying to the US Congress about the national debt, the size and growth of which he deliberately understated. Thanks to his backers, he was never charged... Of course, Lew has his BA from Harvard and JD from Georgetown, which accounts for his success on behalf of the leisure class.

Penny Pritzker, Obama's Secretary of Commerce (2013-2016) received her BA from Harvard and JD and MBA from Stanford. She is a Chicago billionaire, who served as National Financial Chairperson for Barack Obama's 2008 presidential campaign, and was National Chair of his 2012 campaign. Pritzker has been a major player among prominent Chicago Jews ensuring that their candidate Obama 'got it right' on US-Israel relations. Despite having been fined $460 million by the US Treasury Department for predatory banking (Pritzker's Superior Bank of Chicago had fleeced millions of poor and middle class household mortgage holders and investors of billions of dollars of their assets), a grateful Obama named Penny Pritzker as his Secretary of Commerce. She quickly teamed up with Froman and Lew in promoting the free trade agreements that have thoroughly undermined US regulations protecting labor and the environment. Billionaire Pritzker and her partners have been fabulously successful in globalizing profits for the elite while socializing the cost of corporate flight abroad onto the backs of the US working and middle classes.

Dr. Michael Froman, Obama's Chief Trade Negotiator, has a BA from Princeton, a JD from Harvard and PhD from Oxford. Prior to heading up Trade, Froman served under Bill Clinton in Treasury and was a National Security Adviser to President Obama. He actively pushed for the Obama's program of expansive domestic police state surveillance. He is also the principal author and promoter of the Trans-Pacific Partnership, which includes 11 Pacific nations and is designed to marginalize and encircle China. Purported to be a trade partnership, TPP may jeopardize the profits of over 500 major US MNC with investments in China and the US multi-hundred-billion-dollar trade relation. Froman is one of the major architects of Obama's pivot to Asia, which has heightened military tensions and threatens the entire West Coast economies heavily dependent on China trade.

Not to be outdone by other luminaries in the 'economic quintet', Lawrence Summers had been President at Harvard University until he was booted out by a resounding no confidence vote by the faculty, despite the efforts of Zionist academics and trustees who stuck by their 'golden boy'. Summers, along with co-religionist Alan Greenspan (it has been so hard to find any competent Gentiles to steer the US economy), was one of the prime authors of the deregulatory financial policies leading to the 2008-09 financial-economic crash. This crushing success caused double-digit unemployment, three million household foreclosures and forced a trillion dollar bank bailout down the gagging throats of the US taxpayers.

Summers led the charge on the successful repeal of the New Deal's Glass-Steagall Act, a venerable Depression era legislation designed to prevent banks from speculating with their depositors' savings—which the banks promptly did after the repeal.

As Under-Secretary of Treasury in 1993, Deputy-Secretary in 1995 and Treasury Secretary in 1999, the Harvard and MIT-diploma-laden Summers advised the vodka-soaked 'experts' around Boris Yeltsin to privatize the Russian economy, resulting in the pillage by gangster-oligarchs of over $500 billion dollars in public properties, banks and natural resources, and providing significant profits for a score of Harvard-based 'advisers'.

As President of Harvard, he attributed the absence of women scholars in science, mathematics and engineering to their lack of 'high-end' intellectual capacity (ignoring centuries of ingrained discrimination) and he trivialized the academic work of Afro-American scholar, Cornel West, causing him to leave and join Princeton. His denigration of a major African-American scholar was in line with his views on Africa while at the World Bank where he advocated shipping toxic waste because, 'I've always thought that the under-populated countries in Africa were vastly under-polluted."

After alienating women and African Americans, Summers spearheaded a vitriolic attack on any and all campus critics of the state of Israel. He targeted student leaders of the peaceful Boycott, Divestment and Sanctions movement as 'anti-Semites' or 'self-hating Jews', using the University Presidential bully platform to silence opponents of his pro-Israel politics. Eventually, he was ousted from office by an overwhelming faculty vote ostensibly for his financial 'conflict of interests' related to his Yeltsin-era dealings with mega-swindler Andrei Shleifer whose shady deals in Russia's privatization orgy made some Harvard officials very wealthy.

Self-promoted as academic spokesman for the

American worker, Robert Reich received his JD at Yale Law School and taught at Harvard. He served as Labor Secretary under Clinton (1993-97). During Reich's tenure, labor union membership steeply declined, laws prohibiting worker organizing were tightened, and the minimum wage became a minimum survival wage. Reich hung on to his Cabinet position even after the North American Free Trade for the Americas (NAFTA} was approved, destroying over two million once secure American manufacturing jobs. He hung on as President Clinton carpet bombed the renowned worker self-managed factories of Yugoslavia. He kept his luxurious office in Washington after Clinton bombed Sudan's principal factory for the production of vaccines and antibiotics leaving millions of children and adults without basic vaccines and medicines. Reich kept 'mum' even as Haiti was invaded and a harsh neoliberal anti-worker agenda was imposed to permit the democratically elected President Aristide to return to office.

While domestic inequalities deepened and economic deregulation extended, Reich remained in office. Reich ignored Israeli violence against Palestinian labor unions and workers, backing Clinton's 'carnal relation' with Tel Aviv.

After years of devastation against workers at home and abroad, Reich left Washington for a cushy $243,000-a-year appointment at UC Berkeley where he teaches two hours a week assigning his own op-ed columns in the mass media as reading material. When not engaged in such strenuous scholarship, Reich has managed to churn out books 'critical of neoliberalism, inequality and social justice'. Crying all the way to the bank, this intellectual for the oppressed worker has to manage the $40,000 he is paid for each 45 minute speech on the lecture circuit.[1] On an hourly basis, Reich earns 6 times more than the average US corporate CEOs he now denounces.

Conclusion

From our discussion it is clear that there is a profound disparity between the stellar academic achievements of Israel-First officials in the US government and the disastrous consequences of their public policies in office. The ethno-chauvinist claim of unique merit to explain the overwhelming success of American Jews in public office and in other influential spheres is based on a superficial reputational analysis, bolstered by degrees from prestigious universities. But this reliance on reputation has not held up in terms of performance—the successful resolution of concrete problems and issues. Failures and disasters were not just overlooked; they have been rewarded.

After examining the performance of top officials in foreign policy, we find that their assumptions (often blatant manipulations and misrepresentations) about Iraq were completely wrong; their pursuit of war was disastrous and criminal; their 'occupation blueprint' led to prolonged conflict and the rise of terrorism; and their pretext for war was a fabrication derived from their close ties to Israeli intelligence in opposition to the findings US intelligence. Their sanctions policy toward Iran has cost the US economy many billions while their pro-Israel policy cost the US Treasury (and taxpayers) over $110 billion over the last 30 years. Their one-sided Israel-First policy has sabotaged any a two-state resolution of the Palestinian-Israeli conflict and has left millions of Palestinians in abject misery. Meanwhile, the disproportionate number of high officials who have been accused of giving secret US documents to Israel (Wolfowitz, Feith, Indyk and Pollard, etc.) exposes what really constitutes the badge of merit in this critical area of US security policy.

The gulf between academic credentials and actual performance extends to economic policy. Neoliberal policies favoring Wall Street speculators were adopted by such strategic policymakers as Alan Greenspan, Ben Bernanke and Lawrence Summers. Their leadership rendered the country vulnerable to the biggest economic crash since the Great Depression with millions of Americans losing employment and homes. Not only did they play a role in creating the conditions for the crisis, their solution also compounded the disaster by transferring over a trillion dollars from the US Treasury to the investment banks, as a taxpayer-funded bailout of Wall Street. Under their economic leadership, class inequalities have deepened; the financial elite has grown many times richer. Meanwhile, wars in the Middle East have drained the US Treasury of funds, which should have been used to serve the social needs of Americans and finance an economic recovery program through massive domestic investments and repair of our collapsing infrastructure.

The trade policies under the leadership of this 'meritocratic' elite have been an unmitigated disaster for the majority of industrial workers, resulting in huge trade deficits and the deskilling of low paid service employment, with profound implications for future generations of American workers. It is no longer a secret that an entire generation of working class Americans has descended into poverty with no prospects of escape except through narcotics and other degradation. On the flip side of the winners and losers, US finance capital has expanded overseas with acquisition and merger fees enriching the 0.1% and the meritocratic officials happily rotating from their Washington offices to Wall Street and back again.

If economic performance were to be measured in terms of sustained growth, balanced budgets, reductions in inequalities, and the creation of stable, well-paying jobs, the economic elite (despite their self-promoted merits) have been absolute failures.

However, if we adopt the one percent criteria for success, their performance looks pretty impressive: they bailed out their banking colleagues, implemented destructive free trade agreements, and opened up overseas investments opportunities with higher rates of profits than might be made from investing in the domestic economy.

If we evaluate foreign policy 'performance' in terms of US political, economic and military interests, their policies have been costly in lives, financial losses and military defeats for the nation as a whole. They rate summa cum lousy.

However if we consider their foreign policies in the alternative terms of Israel's political, economic and military interests, they regain their summa cum laudes! The war against Iraq destroyed an opponent of Israel's ethnic cleansing of Palestine. The systematic destruction of the Iraqi civil society and state has eliminated any possibility of Iraq recovering as a modern secular, multi-ethnic, multi-confessional state. Here, Israel made a major advance toward unopposed regional military dominance without losing a soldier or spending a shekel! The Iran sanctions authored and pushed by Levey and Cohen served to undermine another regional foe of Israeli land grabs in the West Bank, even if it cost the US hundreds of billions in lost profits, markets and oil investments.

By re-setting the criteria for these officials, it is clear that their true 'merit' correlates with their successful policies on behalf of the State of Israel, regardless of how mediocre their performances have been for the United States as a state, or its people. All this might raise questions about the nature of higher education and how performance is evaluated in terms of the larger spheres of the US economy, state and military.

What we suggest is that degrees from prestigious universities and the highest awards have prepared academic high achievers to serve the elites but not the workers; to empower the financiers but not the producers. These years of training and achievement have certainly not prevented destructive foreign loyalties from undermining the greater society, nor have they taught basic civic virtues and egalitarian values. Prestigious universities recruit and train graduates in the mold of the dominant elites and increasingly narrow ethno-classes. They purge, intimidate and marginalize effective critics of Wall Street and of the State of Israel, the two major success markers that derive from an increasingly insulated ethno-chauvinist power configuration. Indeed, the question might arise as to whether the disproportionate rise to the top of academia, government and finance hierarchies by pro-Israel Jews has less to do with their effective practical knowledge and democratic values and more to do with their affiliation with the political and economic power that revolves around the one percent, which is played out first in academia, and then in the larger political and economic spheres to the detriment of the vast majority.

The assessment of whatever intrinsic intelligence may exist can be blinded and distorted by an irrational predisposition towards racial-ethnic superiority: the results have been stupid and destructive policies imposed by self-congratulatory, self-contained collectivities with absolutely no accountability for their failures.

Epilogue

The prestigious degrees and awards may account for the appointments but they don't explain the complete absence of any evaluations, or firings or even punishment for failed policies. There have been no consequences for the authors of broken economies, impoverished workers, prolonged losing wars, lies and fabrications of data leading to war, and the passing of confidential state documents. Why have the perpetrators continued to receive promotions in the face of policy failures, going through the revolving doors to appointments to the World Bank, positions in the 'best' universities (to the exclusion of real independent scholars) and lucrative seats in investment banks after their policies have shredded the domestic economy?

Don't the deaths and maiming of millions of Iraqis, Palestinians, Syrians and Libyans, and the tens of millions of desperate refugees, resulting from their foreign policies, warrant a pause in their continued hold on power and prestige, if not outright condemnation for crimes against humanity?

Endnotes

1   "Economist Mark Perry Calls Out Robert Reich For Charging Up To $100K For Speeches," Business Insider, October 30, 2012 <http://www.businessinsider.com/mark-perry-robert-reich-2012-10>

INDEX

1%, the, 69, 123, 239
0.1%, the, 26, 27, 244
9/11 57, 128, 129, 139

A

Abrams, Elliot, 128, 234, 235
Adelson, Sheldon, 62
Afghanistan, 12, 20, 29, 35, 54, 58, 60, 62, 90, 94, 99, 109, 117, 125-128, 130, 131, 138-141, 151, 152, 234-237
African Americans, 27, 31, 47, 59, 241
AIPAC, 51, 154, 219, 222, 233, 237, 238
al-Assad, Bashar, 21, 54, 175, 181, 208, 209
Anti-Semitism, 217, 219
Argentina, 12, 13, 46, 68, 75, 76, 78, 93-95, 97, 103-105, 107, 109, 113, 122, 144, 175, 178, 179, 183, 184, 186, 199, 203, 205
Asian Infrastructure Investment Bank (AIIB), 136, 157, 159, 166, 168, 169

B

Balkans, the, 18, 23, 75, 126
Billionaires, 17, 30, 34, 35, 50, 55, 57, 61, 62, 77, 80, 98, 102, 108, 113, 114, 176, 191, 207, 208, 223, 227, 232, 239
Black Lives Matter, 43, 44
Blackwell, Robert, 162ff
Bloomberg, Michael, 57
Brazil, 12, 13, 75, 76, 78, 93-95, 97, 103-105, 107, 109, 113, 157, 168, 175, 189, 190, 196, 197, 199, 203
BRICS, 96, 136, 157, 159, 168
Bush, George W., 20, 26, 27, 33, 34, 47, 51, 52, 61, 127, 222, 234, 235, 237

C

Caceres, Berta, 60
Camdessus, Michel, 122
Canada, 83, 84, 113, 114, 173, 221
Carter, Ashton, 135, 137, 162, 224
Chavez, Hugo, 20, 180, 184, 203
Chechens, 143, 176, 185, 186, 207, 209
Chertoff, Michael, 57
China, 12, 23, 24, 29, 60, 67-70, 77, 80, 81, 82, 86-88, 94-98, 100, 109, 112, 113, 116-118, 126, 135-138, 146-148, 150, 151, 156-159, 161-171, 175, 177, 178, 182, 183, 185, 186, 211, 224-226, 240
CIA, 92, 144

Class, 27, 32-34, 43-46, 48-49, 67, 69, 71-75, 77-81, 83, 99, 102-105, 107, 112, 118, 122, 123, 139, 152, 153, 190, 191, 196, 199-202, 207, 239, 240, 244, 246
Class struggle, 107, 112, 191, 194, 195, 199
Clinton Foundation, 22
Clinton, Bill, 18, 33, 227, 237, 240
Clinton, Hillary, 11, 17-24, 27, 35, 38, 44, 45, 50-63, 99, 100, 129, 133, 227
Commodities, 100, 106, 180, 196, 200
Corruption, 39, 46, 63, 67, 76-79, 90, 91, 93-95, 100-102, 105, 108, 114, 123, 134, 139, 141, 142, 145, 173, 176-178, 191, 193, 195, 197, 202, 203, 233
Council of Foreign Relations (CFR), 161ff
Crimea, 22, 100, 101, 108, 117, 134,
Cuba, 47, 92-94, 112, 113, 146, 206, 210

D

Democratic Party, 11, 25, 28-35, 37-45, 48, 49, 52, 56, 58, 59, 62-64, 219
Donbass, 22, 100, 101, 107, 125, 134, 157, 177, 185
Drones, 99, 153

E

Ecuador, 94, 199, 201
Egypt, 36, 89, 90, 99, 109, 110, 113, 115
Extreme right, 73, 103
Fascism, 46, 50-55, 62, 70, 72, 195, 204, 206, 210

F

FBI, 57
Feith, Douglas, 235, 236, 243
Feminism, 58
Finance capital, 25, 43, 49, 68, 70, 79, 121, 154, 164, 170, 244, 246
Financial swindles, 13, 27, 35, 46, 68, 72, 80, 100, 102, 121, 123, 190, 218, 226-228, 233, 241
Financial Times, 173ff, 216
France, 13, 70, 72, 73, 75, 76, 78, 81, 84, 115, 121, 122, 210, 217
Froman, Michael, 135, 238-240

G

Gadhafi, Muammar, 21, 36, 59, 63, 132, 133
Garland, Merrick, 229, 230
Germany, 63, 70, 84, 96, 126, 155, 205, 210
Global War on Terror, 127
Globalization, 12, 26, 27, 46, 49, 53, 84
Gorbachev, Mikhail, 114, 163
Greece, 70, 84, 112, 114, 123
Green Party, 64

H

Health care, 29, 36
Hollande, Francois, 70, 71-73, 75
Honduras, 22, 36, 94, 95, 100, 107, 126, 144, 234
Humanitarian intervention, 18, 36, 133

I

IMF, 114, 120-123, 134, 157, 168, 170, 176, 177, 192

Imperialism, 26, 46, 49, 84, 91-93, 124, 207, 228
Indyk, Martin, 237, 238, 243
Iran, 11, 20, 22, 23, 53-55, 58, 67, 89-91, 94, 96, 108, 113, 117, 129, 131, 137, 138, 143, 144, 146, 156, 175, 182, 185, 209, 211, 218, 233-235, 237, 238, 243, 245
Iraq, 12, 18, 20, 26, 29, 33-35, 47, 53, 54, 58, 60, 61, 77, 89, 90, 91, 94, 99, 113, 117, 118, 125, 127-131, 133, 137, 138, 140-142, 145, 147, 152, 155, 174, 182, 186, 204-211, 221, 234-238, 243, 245, 247
ISIS, 23, 47, 52, 71, 91, 138, 141-143, 208, 234, 235
Israel, 35, 38, 50, 51, 54-58, 60, 61, 89-92, 98, 108, 109, 113, 117, 118, 125, 127-135, 137, 141-147, 154, 155, 157, 159, 180, 185, 208, 210, 215ff
Jackson, Jesse, 31-33, 39

J

Japan, 23, 67, 86-88, 135, 136, 150, 157, 166, 170, 183

K

Kagan, Elena, 230
Kagan, Robert, 57
Koch brothers, 57
Kohler, Horst, 122
Kosovo, 85, 91, 126
Kucinich, Dennis, 33-35, 38-40
Kurds, 91, 118, 138, 142, 208

L

Labor, 12, 25, 28, 68-80, 91, 98, 104, 115, 122, 153, 184, 196, 205, 206, 239, 242
Lagarde, Christine, 121, 123
Latin America, 12, 20, 21, 46, 68, 70, 74-78, 81, 83, 88, 92, 94, 95, 97, 98, 100, 101, 103-107, 109, 110, 112, 113, 127, 135, 143-145, 150, 153, 172, 190, 198, 205, 239
Lew, Jake, 47, 135, 238-239
Libya, 12, 21, 29, 35, 36, 40, 53, 54, 58-60, 63, 73, 77, 89, 90, 94, 99, 108, 109, 117, 125, 129, 131-133, 143, 145-147, 151, 155, 186, 234, 235, 237, 247
Lula da Silva, Luiz Inacio, 78, 104, 189, 197, 203

M

Macri, Mauricio, 176, 178, 103, 105
Maduro, Nicolas, 76, 79, 180, 184, 203
Mass media, 17, 24, 27, 53, 58, 69, 79, 101-103, 152, 199, 216, 218, 219, 228, 232, 242
Medicare, 32, 34, 35, 48
Mexico, 22, 46, 51, 68, 74, 92, 95, 233
Middle East, 12, 18, 21, 25, 26, 30, 34, 53, 56, 61, 77, 83, 85, 88-92, 94, 96, 98, 99, 108-110, 113, 1115, 117, 129, 131, 134, 135, 139, 143, 145, 154, 164, 180, 204, 207, 218, 220, 234, 235, 237, 244
Militarism, 20, 23, 47, 116, 124, 159, 165, 228
Modi, Narendra, 161, 167, 168
Mossad, 57, 144, 227
Multinational corporations, 83, 96, 113, 117, 120, 163, 200, 201, 203, 207

Muslims, 24, 26, 46, 48, 50, 53, 57, 176, 216, 218, 234

N

NAFTA, 53, 74, 242
National Endowment for Democracy (NED), 22
National Front, France, 73, 115
Nationalism, 26, 46, 47, 49, 50, 73, 77, 87, 90-94, 100, 107, 113, 117, 119, 129, 133, 137, 139, 142, 152, 172, 184, 204
NATO, 21, 52, 59, 67, 75, 84, 85, 89, 126, 127, 130, 134, 139, 155, 157, 181
Nazis, 19, 100, 107, 109, 115, 157, 204ff
Neoliberalism, 74, 93-95, 97, 101, 104, 106, 109, 11-119, 122, 144, 145, 172, 181, 189-201, 242, 243
Netanyahu, Benjamin, 22, 60, 131, 217, 225, 226, 237
NGOs, 22, 153, 159, 179
Nuclear war, 11, 22, 23, 27, 186
Nuclear weapons, 23, 101, 152, 162, 236
Nuland, Victoria, 22, 57, 176, 177, 179, 224
Nye, Joseph, 148ff

O

Obama, Barack, 12, 20, 23, 27, 34-37, 40, 42, 45, 47, 51-53, 59-61, 97, 99-110, 131, 135, 165-170, 185, 218, 219, 223, 224, 229, 234, 237-240
Occupy Movement, 26, 36, 43, 44, 227
Oligarchs, 27, 40, 45, 46, 63, 68, 80, 93, 94, 100, 107, 109, 114, 123, 157, 177, 182, 205, 241

P

Palestinians, 20, 21, 60, 89-91, 98, 108, 118, 129, 133, 137, 140, 145, 160, 172, 175, 180, 185, 216-218, 222, 231, 234, 237, 238, 242, 243, 245, 247
Paraguay, 22, 92-95, 199
Pensions, 20, 68, 69, 71, 75, 78, 104, 105, 121, 123, 176, 179, 193, 202
Pentagon, 25, 32, 38, 40, 97, 128, 129, 134, 135, 137, 148, 151, 154, 155, 158, 159, 170, 222, 235, 236
Pivot to Asia, 23, 60, 134, 135, 137, 177, 240
Poland, 23, 67, 69, 84, 115, 126
Pollard, Jonathan, 215, 219-223, 228, 243
Popular struggles, 32, 35, 44, 45, 69, 73, 78, 80, 83, 112
Presidents of the Major American Jewish Organizations, 217, 219, 227
Pritzker, Penny, 47, 57, 239
Progressives, 30-32, 36, 37, 39
Putin, Vladimir, 22-24, 47, 52, 61, 114, 175, 176, 182

R

Rato, Rodrigo, 122
Reagan, Ronald, 31, 32, 234
Refugees, 53, 54, 85, 98, 109, 116, 132, 141-143, 181, 186, 205, 236, 247
Regime change, 18, 21-23, 26, 36, 60, 73, 85, 89, 91, 99, 100, 103,

109, 112, 125, 126, 137, 144, 174-176, 185, 208, 237
Republican Party, 12, 25, 26, 30, 35-38, 48-50, 52, 57, 58, 61, 63, 64, 72, 73, 218, 219
Ross, Dennis, 237
Rousseff, Dilma, 76, 78, 104, 105, 203
Russia, 12, 22-24, 52, 61, 67-69, 82, 86, 88-90, 94, 96-98, 100, 101, 108, 113, 114, 116-118, 123, 126, 134, 136, 137, 143, 147, 155, 157, 160, 163, 168, 175, 176, 181, 182, 186, 204, 207, 209, 211, 220

S

Saban, Haim, 57, 58, 60,
Sanctions, 20, 22, 33, 58, 61, 86, 88, 101, 108, 116, 118, 129, 131, 146, 157, 160, 163, 173, 176, 182, 224, 227, 233, 238, 241, 243, 245
Sanders, Bernie, 37, 38, 40, 43-45, 48, 62-64
Sandinistas, 205
Saudi Arabia, 89, 90, 98, 117, 118, 128, 137, 142, 205, 206, 208
Singer, Paul, 57, 144
Snowden, Edward, 27
Social movements, 30, 40, 43, 45, 78, 190, 192, 193
Social Security, 25, 38, 48, 69
Soft power, 149, 152-156, 159,
Somalia, 12, 19, 29, 98, 99, 117, 125, 151, 186
South Africa, 13, 30, 31, 77, 79, 81, 112, 157, 168, 220
Stein, Jill, 64
Strauss-Kahn, Dominique, 122
Summers, Larry, 230, 239-241, 244

Syria, 12, 21, 29, 35, 40, 53-55, 58, 61, 73, 89, 90, 91, 94, 98, 99, 107-109, 115-118, 125, 129, 131, 133, 134, 137, 138, 141-143, 146, 147, 151, 152, 155, 159, 175, 180-182, 185, 186, 204-211, 221, 234, 235, 237, 247

T

Taliban, 90, 99, 117, 127, 128, 139, 237
Tax evasion, 68, 122, 123, 193
Tellis, Ashley, 162ff
Trade unions, 27, 28, 31, 32, 39, 40, 43, 44, 46, 51, 74, 78, 79, 105, 112, 118, 181, 190-195, 206
Trans Pacific Partnership (TPP), 130, 166, 245
Trump, Donald, 17, 18, 24-27, 46-48, 50-55, 57-63
Turkey, 89, 90, 110, 115, 116, 118, 137, 142, 205, 206, 208-210, 216

U

Ukraine, 22. 23. 29. 36, 54, 85, 88, 94, 100, 107, 108, 110, 115-118, 123, 125, 126, 133, 134, 145, 147, 151, 157, 161, 176, 179, 182, 185, 206
US Supreme Court, 47, 229-231

V

Venezuela, 12, 20, 22, 60, 75, 76, 79, 93-95, 100, 103, 105-107, 112, 113, 117, 126, 144, 160, 175, 179, 184, 186, 199, 201, 203

W

Wall Street, 12, 19, 26-30, 32-40, 43, 46-48, 53-58, 62, 99, 165, 170, 172, 173, 178, 184, 225, 233, 244, 246
Wall Street Journal, 27, 173, 184, 225
WASPs, 47, 48, 229-231
Wolfowitz, Paul, 128-130, 235, 243
World Bank, 120, 241, 247
World Trade Organization (WTO), 163

Y

Yellen, Janet, 47, 239
Yeltsin, Boris, 19, 114, 163, 176, 182, 241
Yemen, 12, 21, 35, 40, 54, 61, 89, 90, 98, 99, 107, 108, 113, 115, 118, 125, 131, 137, 138, 151, 153, 186, 208
Yugoslavia, 19, 29, 33, 85, 94, 117, 242

Z

Zionism, 13, 19, 26, 35, 43, 55-59, 61-63, 91, 127-138, 140-147, 154, 172, 180, 215ff